# SCARFACE™

## THE MOVIE SCRIPTBOOK

Written by
Oliver Stone

CW01082305

# SCARFACE

## THE MOVIE SCRIPTBOOK

Written by
Oliver Stone

Book Design by Robbie Robbins
Edited by Justin Eisinger

ISBN: 978-1-60010-095-6
10 09 08 07   1 2 3 4

IDW Publishing is:
Ted Adams, Co-President
Robbie Robbins, Co-President
Chris Ryall, Publisher/Editor-in-Chief
Kris Oprisko, Vice President
Alan Payne, Vice President of Sales
Neil Uyetake, Art Director
Dan Taylor, Editor
Justin Eisinger, Assistant Editor
Tom Waltz, Assistant Editor
Chris Mowry, Graphic Artist
Matthew Ruzicka, CPA, Controller
Alonzo Simon, Shipping Manager
Alex Garner, Creative Director
Yumiko Miyano, Business Development
Rick Privman, Business Development

Special thanks to Cindy Chang and Daniel
McPeek at Universal Licensed Products for
their invaluable assistance.

www.IDWPUBLISHING.com

SCARFACE: THE MOVIE SCRIPTBOOK. JULY 2007. FIRST PRINTING. © 2007 Universal Studios Licensing LLLP. Scarface is a copyright and trademark of Universal Studios. All Rights Reserved. © 2007 Idea and Design Works, LLC. The IDW logo is registered in the U.S. Patent and Trademark Office. All Rights Reserved. IDW Publishing, a division of Idea and Design Works, LLC. Editorial offices: 4411 Morena Blvd., Suite 106, San Diego, CA 92117. Any similarities to persons living or dead are purely coincidental. With the exception of artwork used for review purposes, none of the contents of this publication may be reprinted without the permission of Idea and Design Works, LLC. Printed in Korea.
IDW Publishing does not read or accept unsolicited submissions of ideas, stories, or artwork.

"Enjoy yourself -- every day
above ground is a good day."


ANONYMOUS, MIAMI 1981

1    A PROLOGUE

crawls up the screen -- with Narrator.

                    NARRATOR
            In May 1980, Fidel Castro -- in
            an effort to normalize relations
            with the Carter Administration -
            - opened the harbor at Mariel,
            Cuba with the apparent intention
            of letting some of his people
            join their relatives in the
            United States. Within seventy-
            two hours, 3,000 U.S. boats were
            headed for Cuba. In the next few
            weeks, it became evident that
            Castro was forcing the boat
            owners to carry back with them
            not only their relatives but the
            dregs of his jail population. By
            the time the port was closed
            125,000 'Marielitos' had landed
            in Florida. An estimated 25,000
            had criminal records. This is
            the story of that minority --
            those they call 'Los Bandidos.'

The prologue is shredded diagonally by the
blade of a stiletto and in the empty black
void we:

CUT TO

Opening Montage - Documentary    Footage:

2    THE DISEMBARKATION

from the harbor in Mariel, Cuba. Vessels of
every nature, waving masses, demonstrations...

3     THE CROSSING

      Sun and storm.

4     THE LANDING - KEY WEST

            The flag of the United States. Choppers swooping
            over the ragged coastline of the Keys. Emerald
            waters dotted with fishing trawlers and
            pleasure craft, an "America the Beautiful"
            -type Immigration theme surging over this.

5     THE PROCESSING

            Long lines. Immigration and Nationalization
            Officials, customs, Public Health, FBI, Church
            and Relief Organizations. Babies bawling,
            arguments over paperwork, refugees being
            interviewed by TV news, people crying, people
            eating, families huddled on floors... chaos.

            The music theme continuing in stately calm as
            we:

      CUT TO

6     INT. OFFICE - PROCESSING HALL - AFTERNOON - A FULL
and   and CLOSEUP OF TONY MONTANA
7
            the scar-faced one, in the young angry prime
            of his life. We dwell first on the scar which
            he likes to scratch now and then. We move to
            the eyes, pure in their fury. Finally we
            encompass the face -- the face of a man about
            to explode -- muscle, tissue, brain -- a man
            willing to live or die and on the increment of
            a moment, inflict or receive either one. He is
            clothed in rags crossed with holes, his shoes
            broken cardboard, his hair unkempt, his
            complexion sallow from prison.

Over this:

                              VOICE #1 (O.S.)
                         Okay so what do you call
                         yourself?

                              VOICE #2 (O.S.)
                         Como se llama?

                              MONTANA
                         Tony Montana... you?

                              VOICE #1
                         Where'd you learn to speak the
                         English, Tony?

                              MONTANA
                         *My* old man -- he was American.
                         Sailor. Bum. I always know,
                         y'know, one day I gonna come to
                         America. I see all the movies...

                              VOICE #1
                         So where's your old man now?

                              MONTANA
                         He's dead. He died.
                         Somewhere...

                              VOICE #1
                         Mother?
                              TONY
                         She's dead too.

                              VOICE #2
                         What kind of work you do in
                         Cuba, Tony?

                              TONY
                         This. That. The Army. Some
                         construction work...

                    VOICE #2
          Un hunh. Got any family in the
          States, Tony? Cousins,
          brother-in-law?

                    TONY
          (a beat)
          No. Nobody. Everybody's dead.

                    MAN #I
          Y'ever been in jail, Tony?

                    TONY
          Me jail? No way.

We now reveal three men in civilian clothing
in the dark afternoon light of the little
room. Actually it's a plywood office somewhere
in the processing hall and we hear the din
from the hall over the question and answer.
Two of the men sit around a desk, the Third
Man stands in a corner, staring at Tony, the
most authoritative-looking of the three.

                    MAN #1
          (checking off a list)
          You been in a mental hospital,
          Tony?

                    TONY
          (grinning)
          Yeah, in the boat coming over.

                    MAN #1
          How 'bout homosexuality,
          Tony? You, like men, y'like to
          dress up like a woman?

                    TONY
          (to Man #2)
          Never tried it. What the

fuck's wrong with this guy,
what's he think I am?

                    MAN #2
          Just answer the questions,
          Tony.

The voices of the men remain cool and
collected throughout.

                    TONY
          (to Man #1)
          Fuck no.

                    MAN #1
          Arrested? Vagrancy? Marijuana?

                    TONY
          Never. Nothing. NO... NO.

His eye movements are rapid (over shoulders,
sides, doors) and he does a lot of touching --
objects -- lightly with the tips of the fingers.
Man #3 is stepping forward out of the shadows.

                    MAN #3
          So where'd you get the beauty
          scar?

                    TONY
          This?..
          (scratching the scar, shrugs)
          I was a kid. You should see
          the other kid.
          (a grim chuckle)

                    MAN #3
          And this?

He holds up Tony's hand and indicates the
tattoo between the thumb and second finger --

a heart with the word "Madre" scaled
through it.

                    TONY
        Oh that was for my sweetheart.

                    MAN #3
        Sweetheart?
        (to the other men)
        We been seeing more and more
        of these. It's some kinda
        code these guys used in the
        can. Pitchfork means an
        assassin or something. This
        one's new... You want to tell
        us, Montana or you want to
        take a little trip to the
        detention center?

                    TONY
        Hey, so I was in the can once
        for buying dollars. Big deal.

                    MAN.#3
        That's pretty funny, Tony.

                    TONY
        Some Canadian tourist...

                    MAN #3
        What'd you mug him first? Get
        him outta here!
        (starts to walk out)

                    TONY
        Hey, so I fuck Castro, what's
        it to you? You a Communist or
        something? How would you like
        it they tell you all the time
        what to think, what to do, you
        wanna be like a sheep, like

everybody else. Baa baa? Puta!
You want a stoolie on every
block? You wanna work eight
hours a day and you never own
nothing? I ate octopus three
times a day, fucking octopus
is coming out my ears, fuckin'
Russian shoes are eating
through my feet. Whaddaya
want? You want me to stay
there? Hey, I'm no little
whore, I'm no stinking thief!
I'm Tony Montana and I'm a
political prisoner here from
Cuba and I want my fucking
'Human Rights' just like
President Jimmy Carter says,
okay?...

Silence.

There's a certain eloquence to the man's plea
but it falls on disbelieving ears. One of them
chuckles.

                    MAN #1
          Carter should see this human
          right. He's good. He's very
          good. What do you say Harry?

                    MAN #3
          (walking out)
          I... 'Freedomtown.' Let them
          take a look at him. A long
          look.

                    TONY
          Hey, that's okay, too, Harry.
          No hard feelings.

Man #3 at the door stops, looks back.

                         TONY
            Send me here, send me there.
            This. That. Nothing you can do
            to me Harry, Castro didn't do
            -- nothing...

      That taunting smile on Tony's lips as, to the
      music of the immigration theme, we:

DISSOLVE TO

7-A    INT. FEDERAL BUS - HOUR LATER

            The bus is packed with the harder-looking
            refugee-types. The windows are caged and we
            see INS guards. The noise level is high, like
            a sack of monkeys.

            Manny (Manolo) Ribera's got his feet up on an
            empty seat.

            He's big, strong, handsome, with dashing
            darkly feminine eyes -- younger than Tony, and
            dapper in his cheap clothing. He's eating a
            Baby Ruth candy bar.

                         MANNY
            Seat's taken.

                         TONY
            So I'll sit in your lap.

            Tony pushes his feet off, sits. He takes the
            Baby Ruth out of Manny's hand, peels out the
            bar of chocolate, then returns the empty
            wrapper to Manny,

                         TONY
            So what'd you tell them?

                    MANNY

          I told them what you told me
          to tell them. I told them I
          was in sanitation in Cuba.

                    TONY

          I didn't tell you sanitation.
          I told you to tell them you
          was in a sanitarium, not
          sanitation.

The bus pulling out now.

                    MANNY

          Is that what you told me? You
          didn't tell me that.

                    TONY

          You know if you hadn't opened
          your mouth, they woulda
          thought you were a horse. I
          told you to tell them you had
          TB and was cured.

                    MANNY

          Fuck you Tony...

                    TONY

          You did nothing right. I
          shoulda left you in Cuba.


7-B     EXT. MIAMI FROM BUS - ESTABLISHING SHOT

          of Miami as, to the music of the Immigration
          theme, we:

DISSOLVE TO

8       INT. TONY'S TENT - FREEDOMTOWN - NIGHT (SIX
        MONTHS LATER)

A movie projector... the face of Bogart --
unshaven, paranoid. We're watching a badly
damaged 16 mm print of *The Treasure of the
Sierra Madre*. It's near the end of the film
and he's alone, talking to himself just before
the bandits get him...

The rag-tag audience is noisily yammering
back at the screen, the camera moving past
Manny Ray, chewing gum, hair slicked, eyes in
cat-like repose... to Tony, enrapt, eyes like
an eleven year old, mouth hanging open.

>                    BOGART
> Conscience. Conscience. What a
> thing. If you believe you've
> got a conscience, it'll pester
> you to death. But if you don't
> believe you've got one, what
> can it do to you? Makes me
> sick so much talking and
> fussing about nonsense. Time
> to go to sleep.
> (closes his eyes but not for
> long)

CUT TO

9        INT. TENT - LATER THAT NIGHT

Tony is moving down 23rd Street, the walk
proud and jungle in the rock of the hips and
the cast of the shoulders -- now accompanied
by his handsome compadre, Manny

>                    TONY
> That Bogart, chico, hunh?

>                    MANNY
> Fucking crazy, hunh!

                    TONY
          That gold dust blowing in the
          wind. Y'see Manny, he's always
          looking over his shoulder.
          Hunh? Like me...

He hunches, darting exaggerated looks over his
shoulder, imitating Bogart. Manny laughs. In
his black shirt with zig-zag dots and colors
and the baggy pants and sunglasses, Tony's
starting to look American. He's even got
himself a pop button pinned to his shirt that
says "Fuck Off and Die." And his English rolls
faster off his tongue, his confidence more
pronounced.

                    TONY
          I... don't trust nobody.

                    MANNY
          Yeah all that gold, hunh -- I
          guess you get so crazy you
          never trust nobody no more.

                    TONY
          Never happen to me, chico.
          That's one thing I never gonna
          be. I never gonna be crazy
          like that.

                    MANNY
          Yeah, how do you know...

                    TONY
          I know.

                    MANNY
          I don't know. Sometimes you
          crazy, too, Tony.

                    TONY

     Assholes, I go crazy. You
     Manny, I never go crazy with
     you. You're like my brother, I
     love you!


                    MANNY

     Yeah, sure.


                    TONY

     Hey, c'mon.


Tony playfully punches Manny and they walk on
into the humid night, intersecting a young
punk, Chi-Chi.


                    CHI-CHI

     (to Manny; Spanish)
     Hey Manny.


                    MANNY

     Oye Chi-Chi, what's going
     down.


                    CHI-CHI

     Usual shit. Want some peanuts?
     Pogo's carrying tonight.


                    MANNY

     I don't know, I get all fucked
     up on it...


                    CHI-CHI

     Want some new snatch? A
     pussycat name of Yolanda just
     rolled onto the Boulevard ---


                    MANNY

     Oh yeah, what she look like?

                              CHI-CHI
                   She look like you 'cept she
                   got a snatch.


                              MANNY
                   A real snatch?


                              CHI-CHI
                   You're not kidding. It talks.


          As they chatter, Tony moves on with a movement
          of the head for Manny. "Later."

          He's in the middle of the "Boulevard" where a
          bustling black market in toiletries, clothing,
          cigarettes, and transvestites is conducted
          nightly in the harsh glare of barrack neon.

          He ambles past a bunch of young guys throwing
          a Frisbee, past a "Viva Carter!" proclamation
          in graffiti...


                              TRANSVESTITE
                   (passing)
                   What about you sugar -- you
                   wanna party?


                              TONY
                   (passing her)
                   Yeah with whose cock, honey?


     CUT TO


10   EXT. FREEDOMTOWN GROUNDS - NIGHT

               Tony, five minutes later, in a phone booth,
               in the middle of a bank of them, dozens of
               Marielietos pressing to get in, trying still
               to contact somebody -- anybody -- on the
               outside.

Tony is dialing, his eyes shifting down to the telephone number written in pencil on the back of a snapshot. As he finishes the number, he flips the snapshot over and we see a young girl, about thirteen years old, dark, tiny, fiery, standing together with a dog and Tony, early twenties, in shadow, the fringes of the photo heavily tattered with handling. Tony stares at it, his mind drifting as the phone rings in a distant place. A brief moment of repose we have not yet seen in Tony.

Someone picks up the phone. An older woman's Voice. His expression alters to uncertainty.

                    VOICE
          Yes? Hello? Who is this?

Tony changes his mind, hangs up. Pause. The faces of those in line peer in, the next party raps on the door, but Tony ignores it, slips the snapshot back into the wallet in his pants, then at his own pace, exits the phone booth.

He walks a few beats, his eyes pensive. Then recognizes somebody in another phone booth and goes over.

Angel Frenandez has got the face of one, as he argues on the phone, then hangs up, a desolate look on his face, a worn phone book in his hand.

                    TONY
          Angel, how ya doin'?

                    ANGEL
          You know how many goddamn
          Fernandezes are living in
          fucking Union City? And I
          gotta call every fucking one
          of 'em to find my brother!

                    TONY
          (in passing)
          Don't waste your dime, chico.
          You know your brother hates you.

                    ANGEL
          Go fuck yourself, Tony.

Manny catches up to Tony.

                    TONY
          Whatcha hanging around with
          that hustler for?

                    MANNY
          Hey Chi-Chi's okay, he hears
          things,

                    TONY
          What's he hear I don't hear.

Angel comes over, listens.

                    MANNY
          He hears we got problems.
          Immigration is having these
          hearings, y'know? And they're
          saying nine out of ten of us
          is gonna get shipped back!

                    TONY
          Oh yeah?

                    MANNY
          Yeah. And a lotta shit just
          went down at Indiantown Gap.
          In Pennsylvania. Riots, fires,
          broken heads... things are
          gonna pop here.

                    TONY
          Shit, I coulda told you that.


                    MANNY
          Yeah, so what do you think the
          immigration's gonna do when we
          riot? You think they're gonna
          let us out? They're gonna
          throw away the key, that's
          what.


                    ANGEL
          Oh shit! What's I say. This is
          gonna end bad, muchachos...


                    TONY
          Hey, I tell you guys this
          isn't Cuba here, this is the
          United States. They got
          nothing but lawyers here.
          We're on the television. We're
          in the newspapers. Whatta they
          gonna do -- ship us back to
          Cuba? Castro -- he don't want
          us. Nobody no place wants us
          so whatta they gonna do -- put
          us in a gas chamber so all the
          people can see? They're stuck
          with us, chico -- they gotta
          let us go!


                    MANNY
          Yeah, well, what if we gotta
          sit here another six months,
          hunh?


                    TONY
          You worry too much, mi
          hermano. Like the man
          says,'when you got 'em by

                    the balls, their hearts
                    and minds gonna
                    follow -- hunh?


          Tony winks and walks off.

          The radio is playing hard rock, something like
          Blondie or Benatar from the stoop of a nearby
          barrack. Tony loves the sound and swings into
          it, snapping his fingers and rolling his hips
          like Presley. He back-peddles, smiling at
          Manny and Angel.

                              TONY
                    (in awful imitation)
                    'Oh yeah America! Love-to love
                    you baby, oh yeah!'

     CUT TO

11     EXT. PLAYING FIELD - DAY - TWO WEEKS LATER

          Camera on Tony shuffling and feinting a soccer
          ball in an impromtu game; he's covered with
          sweat, tries a fancy move around a younger kid
          who not only steals the ball away from him but
          manages to lay him flat on his face.

                              TONY
                    (lying there)
                    Aw fuck...

          The game, leaving him behind, shifts
          downfield.

                              MANNY
                    Oye! Tony! C'mon!

          Manny, just arrived at the edge of the field,
          waves him over.

Tony, getting up, brushing himself off, walks
off the field towards him.

                    ANGEL
          (at a distance)
          Hey Tony where ya going?

                    TONY
          I got better-things to do.

                    ANGEL
          Chicken liver, hunh?

                    TONY
          (to Manny)
          Yeah?

                    MANNY
          (looking around)
          Let's walk.

They walk.

                    MANNY
          You ready for the good news,
          cono?

                    TONY
          Yeah.

                    MANNY
          We can be outta here in thirty
          days. Not only that. We got a
          green card and a job in Miami!
          Hunh? We're made, chico, we're
          made?

                    TONY
          Yeah, whadda we gotta do, go
          to Cuba and hit the Beard or
          what?

Angel is walking towards them. Tony signals
him.

                    MANNY
              (shakes his head)
          Forget it. Oh yeah -- there's
          a hundred greenbacks in it,
          for both of us.

                    TONY
              (enthusiastic)
          Hey you're kidding, that's
          great! But Manny, you tell
          your guys Angel gets out with
          us.

As Rebenga, in long-lensed closeup, nervously
smokes a cigarette, eyes roving as the guard
examines his papers.

    CUT TO

13    MONTAGE - THE RIOT - FREEDOMTOWN - DAY

          The visuals are swift, dispassionate and
          documentary-like. The refugees storm the
          barbed wire at the main gate, carrying bricks
          and wooden slats.

                    ALL
              (in unison)
          Libertad! Libertad!

14    NATIONAL GUARDSMEN AND STATE POLICE

    form ranks outside.

15    REFUGEES

    flee through a hole in the fence.

16    GUARDS

      move on them, wielding clubs.

17    SEVERAL REFUGEES

      are scooting down a highway.

18    POLICE DOGS

      on chains are glimpsed.

19    REFUGEES

            throw stones and debris from the rooftop of a
            barrack.

20    REBENGA

            a cigarette in his mouth, nervously hurries
            into a barrack.

21    ANGEL

            tracks him, signals...

22    INSIDE - REFUGEES

            are pulling apart their beds, going for
            the wooden slats. Others set fire to their
            mattresses.

23    THE POLICE AND GUARDS

            are moving through the gates, restoring order.
            Loudspeakers blast. Injured refugees lie
            bleeding on the grounds.

24    AN ENTIRE BARRACK

            now goes up in flames.

25    INSIDE THE BARRACK

          A bewildered Emilio Rebenga grabs his papers
          and valuables.

          Manny runs up on him.

          Rebenga sees him, senses danger, flees down
          the aisle with his satchel, intersecting other
          panicked refugees.

          Manny follows.

          Rebenga stumbles into a bed frame, shatters
          his glasses, then runs on. Into the smoke and
          flame. Out of which Scarface now appears -- in
          his killing wrath.

                          TONY
               Rebenga!

          Rebenga snaps to the sound of the voice.

                          TONY
               (Spanish)
               From the friends you fucked!

          The work is fast. The stiletto punches nine
          quick holes in his lungs and his heart... And
          the figure of death is gone.

          ...And Emilio Rebenga staggers wildly in the
          smoke, uncomprehending eyes encased in broken
          glasses sinking out of frame.

26    EXT. FREEDOMTOWN - DAY

          The riot is over. The grounds are still, smoke
          and debris the aftermath.

DISSOLVE TO

27     INT. PROCESSING ROOM - DAY - A MONTH LATER

An Immigration Officer passes a sheaf of
documents across a desk into a pair of hands.
The camera gliding along a Green Card pinned
to the top of the stack.

It says "ANTHONY MONTANA" and it has picture
and stamps. It's official, as the camera
moves with triumphant immigration theme music
to the face of Mr. Montana examining quite
contentedly the rewards of his efforts.

End of montage. Music continues.

DISSOLVE TO

27-A   EXT. DOWNTOWN MIAMI - SUNNY DAY

The new Miami is rising ubiquitously above
Biscayne Bay, the camera moving past blossoming
skyscrapers, workmen, huge cranes, glass,
mirrors booming upwards into a beautiful blue
Florida sky, fleeced with perfectly white
clouds... past a giant billboard:

HOW ABOUT A MILLION DOLLAR LOAN?
COME TALK TO US...
AT THE BANCO DE MIAMI...
TODAY!

Past banks of glass (Caribank, Banco de
Venezuela, Amerifirst)

Insert a car sticker going by with the image
of the American flag and the reminder: "Will
the last American leaving Miami please bring
the flag?"

Tony and Manny bop along the street in their
hand-me-down clothes, oogling the chicas and
the bodegas (in a plush modern area of Miami).
Boats. Buildings. Cars.

                    TONY
          (looking around)
          Boy -- can you believe this
          place chico?

                    MANNY
          (Spanish)
          Man, they weren't kidding
          around.

                    TONY
          (pointing to a little old man
          walking towards them)
          See that old guy over there?

                    MANNY
          Yeah.

                    TONY
          Millionaire.

                    MANNY
          How do you know?

                    TONY
          Go over there. Ask him gimme
          some money. He'll give you the
          silver right outta his pants --
          that's America man, that's
          what they do here.

                    MANNY
          (almost believing)
          Yeah? Hey Tony catch this tomato.
          (adjusting his pants)
          Ooooh baby doll... (*SEE NOTE)

A hot Cuban girl in heels comes down the
sidewalk towards them with a female friend.
(*SEE NOTE)

                    TONY
          Hey baby what you say?
          (*SEE NOTE)

She looks at him like he was the last thing in
the world she'd say anything to.

Tony waves her off, then changes his mind
and runs up behind her and throws up her
skirt and peeks at her ass. Before she can
react, he hops away laughing as the two
Cuban girls ad-lib Spanish expletives at him.

                    MANNY
          Hey that's not cool, man. You
          wanna score one of these
          chicks, watch me. Mira!

He wiggles his tongue up and down, fast
like a small whirring motor part, then
slips it back into his mouth in the flick
of an eye.

                    TONY
          ...the fuck was that?

                    MANNY
          You didn't see it? You weren't
          looking. Hey you gotta watch
          for it.

Does it again, quickly; it looks like a baby
robin's head peeking out of a nest in his
teeth, then it's gone.

                              TONY
                    What the hell's that for --
                    eating bugs? That's
                    disgustin'.

                              MANNY
                    You think so hunh? Well you
                    don't know shit 'bout chicks
                    chico. When they see this,
                    they *know*. They go *crazy*. They
                    don't resist me.

Does it again. Tony tries but lacks the speed
and agility, provoking Manny's laughter. Manny
double checks himself in a shop window.

                              MANNY
                    (doing it again)
                    Takes practice, mi sangre, but
                    they just love it when you
                    flop that pussy with it...

                              TONY
                    Oooh... cono! How 'bout that
                    one?

Pointing to a tall, cool blonde across the
avenue.

                              MANNY
                    No problem.

27-B   EXT. MIAMI SHOPPING STREET - DAY

        Tony walks right out into the avenue, sticking
        out his arm and stopping traffic. Cars honk
        angrily but he couldn't give a shit.

                              TONY
                    Come on?

Manny follows as Tony now moves across the
opposite lane, a car screeching to a halt in
front of him.

                    TONY
          (points)
          Okay Robert Redford, strut
          your stuff.

The blonde has paused to look in a shop
window.

Manny stops alongside, pretends to look. When
he catches her eyes, he flicks his tongue.

She looks at him, confused, then back into the
window.

Manny looks back at Tony, winks, sidles closer
to her.

Tony, waiting off to the side, catches the
gaze of a somber child, four, toddling along
with it's mom. He makes his own version of a
funny face at the kid who looks back at him
puzzled. Tony produces another face. The kid
now smiles. The mother looks over. Tony
shrugs. She smiles and moves along.

Meanwhile, Manny has moved close to the blonde
and suggests something, his eyebrows raising,
the smile crooked. It takes a moment, then the
blonde smacks him across the face and walks
away.

Tony walks over to him, mocking.

                    TONY
          Pobre hijo de puta -- you got
          it all mixed up. This country
          first you gotta get the money,

then you get the power and
when you got the power, then
you get the women -- and then,
chico, you got the world by
the balls. Por los conjones.

                    MANNY
          There you go talking big again
          man. You don't know shit about
          the world. Who was it got us
          the green card, who got us the
          friends with the connections,
          hunh -- who's getting us a
          job? You or me? Not you man.
          You lucky you have any
          friends. You lucky to have me
          as a friend...

As they walk off, back to camera.

                    TONY
          Yeah, so where's this job?

                    MANNY
          Don't push man, my friends
          gonna take care of everything.

     CUT TO

28   LITTLE HAVANA RESTAURANT - LITTLE HAVANA - NIGHT

     on Southwest 8th Street. "Calle Ocho"...

     The parking lot is crammed with Moby Dick-size
     cars and casual Cubans in sports clothes
     bunched in conversations around their wheels
     or at the ice cream stand.

     The inside is a brightly lit glitter dome with
     fancy mirrors and chandelier effects, Spanish
     in influence, and every table is taken. It

combines the social functions of a family restaurant, cafe, tourist haunt and late-night watering hole for various beasts of prey.

The waitresses move like well-oiled troops along the paths to the kitchen, turning the tables at a speedy rate. The camera following past the pots and the pans and the steam and the yelling cooks -- to the deepest, darkest recess of this dungeon...

...To reveal Tony Montana stubbing grease off the pots and Manny Ray washing a stack of dishes. They're filthy and exhausted. A dish slips through Manny's fingers and crashes to the floor. A look between them suffices to tell us all.

                    TONY
          Your big shot friend better
          come up with something soon. I
          didn't come to America to break
          my fucking back, querido.

                    MANNY
          (equally irritated)
          Hey he's coming okay! What do
          you want?

     CUT TO


29   INT./EXT. LITTLE HAVANA RESTAURANT - NIGHT - HOURS
     LATER

          we are looking through a cubbyhole at the
          diners. Young Cuban guys with chiquitas drift
          in with their fancy clothes, diamonds and --
          the mark of status -- large bodyguards.
          They're out front with the flash, shaking
          hands with friends, kissing, talking loud,
          familiar with the waitresses.

Staring through the smeared window enrapt are Tony and Manny, wiping the sweat off their faces with towels.

>                    MANNY
>           Look at that chick man, wow!
>           Look at them knockers.

>                    TONY
>           Yeah, look at the punk with
>           her. What's he got that I
>           don't got?

>                    MANNY
>           He's good-looking that's
>           what, look at his clothes,
>           flash chico, pizzaz!... a
>           little coke money don't hurt
>           nobody...

>                    TONY
>           Junkie! -- They got no fuckin'
>           character.
>               (looks at his hands)
>           Cono! Look at these... fucking
>           onions! They outta be picking
>           gold off the streets.

His hands are shriveled white from dishwater.

>                    COOK
>               (Spanish)
>           Hey you two, outside! You got
>           company.

>                    MANNY
>           That's him -- El Mono's here!

>                    TONY
>               (contemptuous of the name)
>           El Mono? Shit...

CUT TO

30      EXT. PARKING LOT OUTSIDE LITTLE HAVANA RESTAURANT -
        NIGHT

                Omar Suarez (El Mono -- "The Monkey") is so
                named 'cause he looks like one. Nervous,
                crooked, darting eyes, feverish intelligence,
                constantly smoking a cigarette and coughing
                between words, his face pock-marked and pitted
                like the moon from old acne scars, he cuts a
                skinny figure at the wheel of a big beige
                Coupe De Ville, idling the motor... with him
                is Waldo Rojas eating a large foot and a half
                banana. In contrast he's amiable, heavyset
                with a receding hairline, flashing a lot of
                gold when he smiles.


                              MANNY
                    (leaning in the window)
                    Hey Omar, Waldo, coma esta...
                    my friend I told you about.
                    Tony Montana... Omar Suarez,
                    Waldo Rojas...


                Waldo mumbles something indistinct, Omar just
                stares briefly as Tony hangs back, nodding
                arrogantly. Omar's eyes move back to Manny.


                              OMAR
                    I got something for you.


                              MANNY
                    Oh yeah! That's great... What
                    do we gotta do?


                              OMAR
                    We gotta unload a boat --
                    grass, twenty-five tons --


                                                          33

that's what we gotta do.
You get five hundred each.

                    MANNY

          Okay!
          (to Tony)
          See, what'd I tell you.

                    TONY

          You gotta be kidding! Whadda
          you think we are -- baggage
          handlers?

Omar looks at him some what incredulously as
Tony wipes his hands on his greasy apron as he
talks.

                    TONY

          ...five hundred dollars --
          shit! What'd I do for you guys
          in the slammer, hunh? What was
          the Rebenga hit -- game of
          dominoes or somethin'? You're
          talkin' to important guys here.

                    MANNY

          (shocked)
          Hey Tony, c'mon, it's okay
          Omar, we...

                    TONY

          Shaddup!

Omar sniggers, his eyes shifting to Waldo who
shakes his head and laughs.

                    OMAR

          (to Manny only)
          So what's it with this
          dishwasher, chico? Don't he
          think we coulda gotten some

other space cadet to do
Rebenga -- cheaper maybe.
Fifty bucks?

                    TONY
          (shrugs)
          So why didn't you? And who the
          fuck you calling a dishwasher,
          I'll wipe your monkeyshit
          ass all up and down this
          Boulevard.

Steps forward. Manny grabs him.

                    MANNY
          Hey! -- Tony, Tony...

In the car, Omar looks over at Waldo.

                    OMAR
          Guy's a lunatic, let's go.

                    WALDO
          What about them Indians---

The idea crosses Omar's mind. He buys it,
somewhat amused.

                    OMAR
          Yeah.. . .
          (back to Tony)
          All right, smart ass, you
          wanna make some big bucks? You
          know anything about cocaine?

                    TONY
          You kidding.

                    OMAR
          ...There's a bunch of
          Columbians. Flying in Friday.

New guys. They say they got
two keys for us for openers.
**Pure** coke. In a motel over in
Miami Beach. I want you to go
over there, and if it's what
they say it is, pay 'em and
bring it back. You do that,
you'll make five grand.

               MANNY
(to Tony)
Hey, that sounds great,
Tony...

Tony says nothing.

               OMAR
You know how to handle a
machine gun?

               MANNY
Sure we was in the Army
together.

               OMAR
You're gonna need a couple
other guys...

               MANNY
No problem.

               OMAR
Meet me at Hector's bodega
Friday at noon. You get the
money then. Something happens
to the money, pobrecito,
and my boss gonna stick
your head up your asses
faster'n a rabbit gets
fucked.

Throws the remains of his cigarette at their
feet and pulls the Coupe De Ville out of the
lot.

                    TONY
          I'm scared.

                    MANNY
          (relieved)
          Tony you're pushin' your luck.

                    TONY
          (walking away)
          You worry too much Manny --
          you're gonna get yourself a
          heart attack one of these
          days.

                    MANNY
          (catching up)
          Yeah, so who are these
          Columbians?

                    TONY
          So what does it matter?

                    MANNY
          So whatcha have that look on
          for when Omar bring it up?

Tony strips off his greasy apron.

                    TONY
          So nothin'. I just don't like
          fuckin' Columbians that's
          what. They're animals!

                    COOK
          (intersecting, Spanish)
          Where you greasers going,

                    hunh, I got plenty of plates
                    here.

                              TONY
                    Wash 'em yourself. I just
                    retired.

          Throws the Cook his apron.

                              COOK
                    (Spanish)
                    What the fuck you gonna do!

                              TONY
                    Look after my investments.

          CUT TO

31    EXT. MIAMI BEACH - DAY - MOVING SHOT

          The somewhat run-down, art-deco cheaper hotels
          of South Miami Beach. The porches are filled
          with senior citizens playing cards, reading
          papers, staring, slowly walking the street.

          The ramshackle sedan, jammed with Tony and his
          gang, rattles past. It's a beaten-up black and
          blue Monte Carlo, jacked up on its springs
          with dune buggy threads and needing paint.
          You'd arrest these guys on sight.

32    INT./EXT. TONY'S CAR - MIAMI BEACH - DAY

          seen from the inside of the sedan. Tony turns
          down the salsa beat on the radio, smoking a
          cigarette tensely. Driving is Manny. In the
          dilapidated backseat are Angel, the baby-faced
          punk, and Chi-Chi, both from Freedomtown.

          Manny, reflecting the tension, whistles a
          vapid series of notes under his breath as he

waits for a light to change.

>           MANNY
>       Hey look at that chick, hunh?
>       Lookit those tits man, she's
>       begging for it!

At the curb, an old crone hunchbacks her way
in front of the teenage chick, who is coming
off the beach in a bikini, blocking her off.

>           CHI-CHI
>       (looking over)
>       Whatta you crazy? She's 103
>       years old.

>           MANNY
>       Not her stupido! Her...

Camera revealing the teenager.

>           TONY
>       (the light changing)
>       Drive, willya.

>           MANNY
>       (mocking)
>       Sure, sure. Not to worry, Tony
>       -- You get a heart attack.
>       (looking in the rearview
>       mirror)
>       Angel, whatcha wearing the
>       face for?

>           ANGEL
>       (tense, making light of it)
>       Ah, it's okay. I just y'know
>       forgot to make an offering.
>       I was supposed to go by the
>       madrina today.

                    MANNY
          You still going to that
          cuncha?


                    ANGEL
          She knows her shit. She
          talks to Yemaya and Chango
          like nobody y'ever heard.


As he talks, Angel fingers a Negrita charm
hanging around his neck -- Chango, God of Fire
and Thunder, his black face tilted at a carnal
angle. Sharp teeth glinting, his eyes rolling
in orgasmic imagery, his head crowned with
gold. Many of the Marielitos in the film will
be wearing this, also pendants with an eye to
ward off the evil spirits, red and white
beads, red kerchiefs, black hand charms,
silver-bangled bracelets, etc., all relating
to their Afro-Catholic spiritualism.


                    MANNY
          (making fun)
          Yeah, Chango looking out for
          us, Angel?


                    ANGEL
          Chango looking out for all the
          'bandidos' everywhere. But you
          gotta pay him his dues, y'know.
          You gotta let him know you
          respect him. You don't, Chango
          -- he gets pissed an...


                    TONY
          (angry)
          Hey, shaddup -- all of ya! I
          told you before I don't go for
          that mystical voodoo shit.
          That's for the old cunchas
          waving their rooster cocks in

some dark alley. There's no
gods, there's no Chango --
nowhere! You make your own
luck. So shaddup and act like
you're in the United States
here.

Silence. Through the windshield, the sign of
a motel -- THE SUN RAY -- is coming closer.

                    TONY
          Okay, this is it. Pull over
          across the street.

The motel is coming closer in silence.


                    TONY
          (to Manny)
          Money stays in the trunk
          'till I come out and get it.
          Me. Nobody else. If I'm not
          out in fifteen minutes,
          something's wrong. I'm in
          Room 9. You ready, Angelito?

                    ANGEL
          Sure thing.

As Manny pulls the car up, they pull out an
Ingram Model-10 machine pistol with folding
butt and suppressor, ten inches of kill power
capable of firing 1100 rounds a minute -- it
can be slipped into a man's purse, it's in
vogue. Tony getting out, to Angel:

                    TONY
          Let's go...

CUT TO

33     EXT. SUN-RAY MOTEL - DAY

          Tony and Angel come slowly, gingerly down
          an exterior corridor to a room marked "9".
          Nodding to Angel who remains in the stairwell
          with the Ingram machine pistol, Tony knocks.
          Pause.

34     EXT. TOAD'S MOTEL ROOM - DAY

          The door's opened casually by an ugly, squat
          five-foot-four-inch Columbian, "The Toad".
          He's in his forties, sports shirt hanging over
          his polyester pants, old acne scars on his
          face, like Omar; he's good-natured, a nice
          guy, he smiles.

                         TOAD
                   Hey, oye amigo...

          Spreading his arms in such a fashion to
          indicate he's clean.

35     INT. TOAD'S MOTEL ROOM - DAY

          Tony, stepping into the conventionally tasteless
          orange and blue motel room (with heavy blue
          drapes blocking the windows), spreads his
          hands in a similar posture indicating he too
          is not carrying; but this is only symbolic,
          it's not meant to be a body search.

                         TONY
                   (as he steps in)
                   How you doing amigo...?

          The other person in the room is a tough-
          looking little dark Columbian chick with
          expressionless eyes, red fingernails, and
          short boy-cut hair, "The Lizard"; she's tinier
          than the Toad, about five-two.

The Toad looks around the corridor, eases the
door closed.

> TONY
> (checking out the room)
> Mind leaving the door open so
> my brothers know everything's
> okay... okay?

Toad shrugs and readjusts, leaving it open a
few inches, the conversation clipped and nervous throughout the scene.

> TOAD
> Sure, no problem... This is
> Marta.

> TONY
> Hello, Marta.

She nods woodenly, stays across the room.
Behind her, the television set is on to
the Cable Newswatch. The protagonists
intermittently flick their eyes to it,
soothing the tension.

> TOAD
> I'm Hector...

Pause.

> TONY
> Yeah. I'm Tony. So Omar says
> you're okay.

> TOAD
> Yeah, Omar's okay.

> TONY
> You know Omar.

                    TOAD
          Omar, yeah, I talk to him on
          the phone.

                    TONY
          Okay...

                    TOAD
          Okay... so you got the money?

                    TONY
          Yeah, you got the stuff?

                    TOAD
          Sure I got the stuff, but I
          don't got it right here with
          me. I got it close by.

                    TONY
          Yeah well I don't got it
          either, I got it close by,
          too.

                    TOAD
          Where, in the parking lot?

                    TONY
          No. How far's your stuff?

Tony paces back towards the door casually, to
check Angel out... The Lizard staring at him.

                    TOAD
          Not far.

Pause. Everything seems okay.

                    TONY
          So what do we do, walk in and
          start over?

                    TOAD
          (changes subject)
          Where you from?

Tony's eyes check out the bathroom.

                    TONY
          What fuckin' difference does
          it make where I'm from?

                    TOAD
          I like to get to know who I do
          business with.

It's like he's stalling for time. The Lizard
has made a move somewhere off-center and is
now sitting on the bed, coiled and always
watching.

                    TONY
          You get to know me when you
          start doing business and not
          fucking around, Hector.

                    TOAD
          Hey I'm just a friendly guy,
          maybe you don't...

                    TONY
          Okay, what's the stall here?
          Your guy late or something?

36    INT. TOAD'S MOTEL ROOM - DAY

          There's suddenly a door slamming somewhere
          outside, then commotion.

                    ANGEL
          Tony!

Tony goes for his cheap handgun when he hears
a frightening female shriek, like a bird.

                    LIZARD
            (slang Spanish)
        Don't! Get up! Now shithead!

She's standing there with a .32 pointed steady
at him, the eyes like angry steel. There's no
mistaking her ability to shoot.

The Toad pulls a 9mm out of the small of his
back, approaches Tony. Angel is shoved into
the room, followed by two more Columbians,
"The Kids". They slam the door, both carrying
Uzis with silencers, neither of them higher
than five-four or older than twenty, with
their straight black Indian hair cut across
their blank eyes, they look like hungry little
pirhana careless about killing, muttering with
the Lizard in fast Columbese slang.

As Toad strips the handgun from Tony:

                    TONY
        Frog face, you just fucked up.
        You steal from me, you're
        dead.

Toad shrugs, he couldn't care less.

                    TOAD
        Yeah, okay, you gonna give me
        the cash or am I gonna kill
        your brother first? 'Fore I
        kill you?

                    TONY
        Try sticking your head up your
        ass. See if it fits.

Toad, completing the body search, rips out
the stiletto taped to the small of Tony's
back. As he mutters something in hard
Columbian slang to the two kids who shove
Angel into the bathroom, producing strands
of thick rope.

Even more worrisome is the chainsaw that the
Lizard now pulls out of the suitcase under
the bed. Toad begins assembling it as Lizard,
still covering Tony with her gun, completes
the deadpan process by turning up the volume
on the television set. The news, not so
ironically in Miami, is about a drug-related
triple-homicide.

CUT TO

37    EXT. SUN-RAY MOTEL - DAY

Chi-Chi sitting at the wheel of the sedan,
parked across the street. Manny paces outside
the car, glances.

38    EXT. SUN-RAY MOTEL - DAY

A small woman -- the Lizard -- steps out in
shadow in the parking lot of the Sun-Ray
across the street, looks around, sees nothing,
casually goes back in.

39    EXT. SUN-RAY MOTEL - DAY

Manny looks at his watch.

CUT TO

40    INT. TOAD'S MOTEL ROOM - DAY

Angel hangs suspended on the ropes from the
top of the shower curtain bar, his legs

straddling the edge of the bathtub. Toad slaps a tape over his mouth.

Tony, covered by the two kids, watches from the lip of the bathroom. He bucks angrily but the two kids ram their pistols up against his temple and pin him to the door.

Angel looks at Tony; the eyes between them steady. They're dead and they know it.

Toad, well-prepared, connects a voltage adapter and extension cord.

> TOAD
> (to Tony)
> You watch what happens to your friend okay? If you don't want this to happen to you, you get the money.

Lizard reenters the room, shakes her head at the Toad who nods and turns on the whirring machine.

The Toad smiles amiably and angles the chainsaw slowly towards Angel.

The two kids press tight against Tony, guns pointed at his brains... o.c. we know what's happening as we hear the chainsaw and we watch Tony's shock and rage.

Lizard has no expression on her face. The machine cuts off.

The Toad steps back from the tub, blood splattered on his shirt, examining his first cut like a butcher. He glances at Tony.

> TOAD
> Now the leg, hunh?

40   CONTINUED

A brief glimpse of Angel slumped by one arm
like a cow on a strap, streaming blood, eyes
conscious and horrified; a terrifying sight.
The chainsaw whirrs once more.

CUT TO

41   EXT. SUN-RAY MOTEL - DAY

Manny, definitely suspecting something now,
moves with Chi-Chi across the parking lot of
the Sun-Ray Motel. They signal and separate.

CUT TO

42   INT. TOAD'S MOTEL ROOM - DAY

The Toad turns off the chainsaw and steps
back, now drenched with Angel's blood, totally
unaffected. He looks at Tony.

Tony glances back at him with fury, tears
involuntarily dotting his eyes.

                    TOAD
          Okay, my 'caracortada',
          you can die too. Makes no
          difference to me.

He nods. The kids shove Tony forward and we
glimpse Angel lying hunkered at his feet in
the bathtub, in the steam of his blood, piss
dead.

CUT TO

43   EXT. SUN-RAY MOTEL - DAY

Manny moves crouched down the exterior corridor, Ingram pistol in hand, past an older couple who pretend not to notice.

At the door of Room 9, Manny waits, listens...

CUT TO

44      INT. TOAD'S MOTEL ROOM - DAY

The kids are starting to strap Tony up to the top of the shower.

The Lizard watches from the lip of the bathroom, impassively.

                    TOAD
          Last chance, carajo?

Tony, devastated, spits in his face.

                    TONY
          Go fuck yourself.

Toad's eyes narrow meanly.

Kid one slaps the tape across Tony's mouth.

Kid two reaches up to tighten the overhead strap to Tony's wrist.

The Toad turns on his chainsaw when suddenly there's a gunshot from the hall.

45      INT./EXT. TOAD'S MOTEL ROOM - DAY

and the door smashes open and Manny barrels through and shoots a surprised Lizard as she raises her pistol. She crashes backwards into the room, wounded. Everything happens very fast now.

Manny is at the lip of the bathroom, he fires
and hits kid one, who is turning, in the neck.

Tony, not tied up yet, spins on kid two and
smashes the unloosened strap across his face,
sending him reeling across the bathroom.

The Toad, chainsaw in hand, slashes at Manny.

Manny fires a burst into him and the Toad
crashes backwards.

Manny now spins into a wall, hit in the side.

The Lizard, wounded on her knees, is firing
her .32 at him. In b-g., the window
simultaneously blows out as Chi-Chi appears
firing a burst with his Ingram.

In sharp f-g., the Lizard crumples forward on
her knees, foaming blood.

Tony, with the tape still stuck across his
mouth, smashes kid two, pinned against the
blood-stained sink, with the stock of his own
Ingram.

In the midst of this, the Toad jumps up,
wounded but with hysterical strength, he tears
out the motel room door gripping the whirring
chainsaw in a reflex action.

Chi-Chi climbing through the window fires at
him.

Meanwhile, kid two, with a rattlesnake life in
him, produces a knife out of nowhere, just
missing Tony's gut by a half-second as Tony
dances back, getting a grip on the machine
pistol.

He blows kid two away point-blank, putting
another ten craters in the mirror of the
now-wrecked motel room.

Tony, yelling, whirls after the Toad.

                    TONY
          I got him!

Manny, holding his side, empties his pistol on
kid one who is still twitching.

Chi-Chi sees Angel, gags.

CUT TO


46      EXT. SUN-RAY MOTEL - DAY

          The senior citizens, playing Mah-Jorigg on the
          porch, mutter in astonishment.

          As the Toad staggers out into the parking lot,
          blood flying, chainsaw in hand, moving like a
          jerky chicken.

          Their eyes follow.

          As Tony comes out, walking after him
          deliberately, eyes set in cold fury, machine
          gun swinging loosely at his side. There's no
          rush, no fear of the police, getting even is
          all that counts. He stands behind the Toad.

                    TONY
               (Spanish)
          Your turn, cabron!...

          The Toad whips around to the voice, eyes stark
          with terror.

Tony empties the clip into the Toad, blowing him apart.

The bystanders just stare, stunned by the ferocity. Then an old lady faints.

The Toad's body lying awkwardly arched in the gutter, Tony turns and with a passing disinterested glimpse at his audience, calmly walks back into the motel; the distance and the light sufficient to conceal Tony's possible identification.

CUT TO

47  SUN-RAY MOTEL - DAY EXT.

Tony intersects Manny, holding his side, with Chi-Chi.

                    TONY
          Manny, you okay?

Manny nods.

                    TONY
          Chi-Chi, get the car. Fast!

                    CHI-CHI
          Si!

48   INT. TOAD'S MOTEL ROOM

Tony strides into the shambles of Room 9, past the bodies and busted furniture to the suitcase on the bed from which the Lizard pulled the chainsaw. The TV news still plays in the corner.

Inside are several kilo-sized stacks of cocaine.

He shuts the suitcase, exits, stops, looks in the bathroom at the corpse of Angel O.C. He goes, stoops, brings Angel's Chango charm into our view, fingers it, tosses it back in the tub. He goes.

CUT TO

49      EXT. SUN-RAY MOTEL - DAY

Chi-Chi has the sedan waiting in the parking lot. Tony hurries out, jumps in, the car speeding off. (Pisalo hasta la tabla -- Step on it.)

Past the senior citizens who are retreating inside their rooms.

The camera swinging to hold on the blue and black Monte Carlo disappearing into the traffic of the Strip as two cop cars come screaming past them from the opposite direction.

CUT TO

50      EXT. LITTLE HAVANA RESTAURANT - PHONE BOOTH - DUSK

The booth is in the busy parking lot, Tony on the phone, Chi-Chi and Manny wait in the sedan.

                    TONY
          Yeah, bunch of cowboys!
          Somebody **fucked up** Omar.

                    OMAR'S VOICE
              (shaken)
          Look, let me check it out
          right away!

                    TONY
          You do that, Omar, you do
          that.

                    OMAR'S VOICE
          You got the money?

                    TONY
          Yeah -- and I got the yeyo.

                    OMAR'S VOICE
          You got the yeyo? Bring it
          here.

                    TONY
          Fuck you. I'm taking it to the
          boss myself. Not you. Me.

                    OMAR'S VOICE
          Okay, okay. All right. Frank's
          gonna wanna see you anyway.
          Look, meet me tonight at
          Hector's at eight.

                    TONY
          Hey Omar...

                    OMAR'S VOICE
          Yeah?

                    TONY
          That was some pick up you sent
          us on.

Pause.

                    OMAR'S VOICE
          What's that mean?

Tony hangs up, walks back to the sedan.

CUT TO

51      EXT. LOPEZ CONDO - SOUTH MIAMI - NIGHT

        on Bricknell Avenue in a swank high-rise
        district adjacent Coconut Grove and Coral
        Gables, the hub of South Miami...

        The doorman shows Omar, Manny, his side
        bandaged, and Tony, carrying the suitcase,
        through giant glass portals, past seriously
        armed security cops in the lobby.

52      INT. LOPEZ CONDO - NIGHT

        A deluxe apartment with the latest in
        electronic security and surveillance, and a
        profusion of mirrors and luxury items... and a
        hefty, Indian-looking bodyguard (Ernie), eyes
        quietly trained like a Doberman pinscher.

        The boss, Frank Lopez, comes down a carpeted
        corridor, dressed for dinner in an expensive
        suit and shoes, somewhat preoccupied as he
        greets Tony, then Manny with a phony effusion
        of warmth. He's of Cuban-Jewish extraction,
        now Americanized in a rough and handsome sort
        of way, on the heavy side, the face going
        slightly soft, but the eyes and bulk
        carrying an odor of danger about him.

                        LOPEZ
                How ya doing, Tony? Glad to
                meet you. How 'bout a drink?

                        TONY
                Mr. Lopez... real pleasure.

                        LOPEZ
                Call me Frank, Tony. Everybody
                calls me Frank. My Little

                    League team, even the
                    prosecutors 'round town,
                    they all call me Frank.

                              TONY
                    Okay Frank.

Frank shakes hands with Manny.

                              LOPEZ
                    Howya doing?

                              MANNY
                    (awed)
                    ...Fine yeah.

                              TONY
                    Manny Ray, he was with us on
                    the job.

                              LOPEZ
                    (to Manny)
                    I hear you caught one?

Manny shrugs, works his arm, showing us the
wound doesn't bother him too much.

                              MANNY
                    Just the flesh. Went right
                    through.

                              LOPEZ
                    (heading for the bar)
                    Yeah, Omar here tells me good
                    things about you boys.

                              TONY
                    (glances at Omar)
                    Yeah. Omar's terrific.

                    LOPEZ
          Not to mention of course the
          nice job you guys did for me
          on that Commie sonufabitch
          Emilio Rebenga.


                    TONY
          You don't have to mention it.
          That was fun.


                    LOPEZ
          (smiles, likes the kid's
          balls)
          Scotch? Gin? Rum?


                    TONY
          Gin's fine.


                    LOPEZ
          (pouring)
          Yeah, I need a guy with steel
          in his balls. I need him close
          to, me, a guy like you Tony --
          and your compadre here.


                    TONY
          Yeah... well.


Still a little overwhelmed by the opulence of
the place, his clothes feeling narrow and
cheap on him, Tony steps forward and puts the
suitcase up on the bar with the gin, which
Lopez passes to him, eyeing the suitcase.


                    TONY
          ...that's it. That's the two
          keys. Angel died 'cause of
          this shit. And here's the
          money.
          (produces the money)
          It's my gift to you -- from me.

Pause. Lopez shakes his head, sighs.

                    LOPEZ
          It's too bad about your
          friend, Tony, if people'd do
          business the right way,
          there'd be no fuckups like
          this...

He glances hard at Omar who squirms.

Without opening it, Lopez signals the
bodyguard who takes the suitcase and the
money from under Tony's nose.

                    LOPEZ
          Don't think I don't appreciate
          this gesture, Tony. You find
          in this business, you stay
          loyal you move up and you move
          up fast. Salud!

They drink the toast. With their eyes.

                    LOPEZ
          Then you find out your biggest
          headache's not bringing in the
          stuff but figuring out what to
          do with all the goddamn cash.
               (drinks)
                    TONY
          Yeah, I hope I have that
          problem some day.

Lopez looks, distracted, down the corridor
from which he came, to Ernie, the bodyguard.

                    LOPEZ
          Where the hell's Elvira? Go
          get her, will you, Ernie?

The big bodyguard exits smoothly.

                    LOPEZ
          (to the others)
          The broad spends half her
          life dressing, the other
          half undressing.

                    TONY
          I guess you gotta catch her in
          the middle, hunh?

Lopez laughs.

                    LOPEZ
          Yeah. When she's not looking -
          What do you say guys, to a
          little food?
          (finishes his drink at his
          impatient pace)

                    TONY
          Yeah sure, I could eat a
          horse.

                    ERNIE
          Here she comes, Mr. Lopez.

53    TONY

          looks up, his eyes tumbling on the most
          beautiful blonde he's ever seen. The lady is
          coming down the glassed-in elevator adjusting
          her $10,000 Yves St. Laurent burgundy dinner
          dress.

                    LOPEZ
          Oooh sweetheart, you look like
          a million bucks.

She doesn't answer, her eyes flicking disinterestedly over Tony and Manny, knowing what the evening's going to be and not too happy about it.
...........................................

                    ALTERNATIVE

                    LOPEZ
          Where you been baby, it's ten
          o'clock, I'm hungry.

                    ELVIRA
          You're always hungry, you
          should try starving.

Lopez laughs.
...........................................

                    LOPEZ
          I want you to meet a friend of
          mine. Tony Montana...
          Elvira... Manny Ribera.

                    ELVIRA
          Hello.

                    TONY
          Uh... hi.

                    MANNY
          (equally impressed)
          Yeah, hi.

                    ELVIRA
          I assume we're going to be a
          fivesome. Where are we having
          dinner?

                    FRANK
          Oh, I thought we'd eat at the
          Babylon.

                    ELVIRA
          Again? If anyone wanted to
          assassinate you, you wouldn't
          be too hard to find.

                    FRANK
          (coming toward her, laughing)
          Me? Who'd want to kill me? I
          got nothing but friends.

                    ELVIRA
          You never know, do you? Maybe
          the catcher on your Little
          League team.

Neatly avoiding his intended smooch, she slips
by him towards the door, her throat flashing a
$20,000 strip of jewelry.

                    ELVIRA
          Come on, Frank, let's go.

Tracking a cool, polished hauteur, she exits
the apartment.

Lopez, after a pause, snaps at his men.

                    LOPEZ
          Okay, let's go.

     CUT TO

54   EXT. THE BABYLON CLUB - NIGHT

     We know this is no workingman's dive when
     Lopez piles them out of his Rolls, and the
     carhops are moving Bugattis, Lamborghinis
     and Corniches in a long snaking line down the
     driveway. Single girls in high-collared silver
     lamé jumpsuits with cinched waists, prowl like

big glistening tents back and forth across
the entry doors, rich young coiffed playboys
in their Porsches honking their horns in
appreciation. Brain drain.

55      INT. BABYLON CLUB - NIGHT

The interior is built like three or four plush
apartments that run together on three separate
levels with imaginative angles, mirrors,
swimming pool, bars, twenty-piece band,
hundreds of tropical plants, dance floor,
video games, computers and a restaurant. It's
a lavish fun spot that will play a central
role in the film, a drug dealer haven and
nighttime capital of South America.

The crowd, a combination of Caucasian and
Latin, is mostly young, rich and happy and
a lot of them coked; the girls, upperclass
in sleek dresses, trim figures, heels, hats,
sensuous bodies, yell as they dance to a
black American music beat "Celebrating" or
"Partying Down Tonight"...

The waitresses, mostly blondes, wear little
Coca Channel hats pinned to their heads and
the barest pants with hose and high heels.

Rich young guys with a lot of gold and
diamonds on their necks and hands huddle
briefly in groups or chat.

Down at the vid games are younger chicks
in jeans and tough-looking tank tops with
"Motherfuckah" and "Fuck Me" written on them.
Manny's coming from the toilets, tries to
pick one of them up.

                    MANNY
          So whaddaya say, hunh?

He flashes his tongue. She looks at him, amused.

                    CHICK
          You got a buck?

                    MANNY
          Sure I got a buck, whaddaya
          think I am, poor?

                    CHICK
          (indicates the machine)
          Put it in, let's play.

                    MANNY
          I had other things in mind.

                    CHICK
          You check out on this and
          we'll talk about other things.

                    MANNY
          (looks off, concerned, then
          confronts the complex machine}
          Fuck, how do you play this
          thing?

     CUT TO

56   INT. BABYLON CLUB

          Frank Lopez, intoxicated, takes his heart pill
          with a slug of champagne. He sits next to
          Tony, who is agog at all this wealth. Omar and
          Ernie look on. Elvira is in conversation with
          a girl friend who has stopped by. They're
          sitting at the best table in the place,
          finishing up a giant meal. The empty spot
          belongs to Manny.

                         LOPEZ
          (to Tony)
          ...Over there that's Ronnie
          Echeverria. Him and his
          brother Miguel they got a big
          distribution set-up here to
          Houston and Tucson...

Their point of view -- Ronnie Echevarria,
powerful, competent-looking man in
conversation with a party of people.

                         LOPEZ
          That guy there, in the purple
          shirt -- Gaspar Gomez. Bad
          news. Stone killer there ever
          was one. Stay away.

Their point of view -- Gaspar Gomez at a table
with another guy and gorgeous woman.

                         LOPEZ
          ...the fat guy, with the
          chicas is Nacho Contreras --
          El Gordo. Wouldn't know it
          to look at him but he's got
          more cash than anybody in
          here. A real haza...

Their point of view -- El Gordo is fat,
dressed like a cheap slob and playing up to a
bunch of chicas.

                         LOPEZ
          ...you know what a haza is,
          Tony?

                         TONY
          'Haza'? No Frank, what's a
          haza?

                    LOPEZ
          It's Yiddish for pig. It's a
          guy he's got more'n what he
          needs, so he don't fly
          straight anymore, y'know.
          That's the problem in this
          business, Tony, there's too
          many 'hazas' and they're
          the ones you got to watch out
          for. If they can fuck you
          outta an extra dime, they'll
          rip you and flip you and then
          fuck you with a stick for the
          pure pleasure of it. See it
          all comes down to one thing,
          Tony boy, never forget it!
          Lesson number one -- don't
          underestimate the other guy's
          greed.

                    ELVIRA
          Lesson number two -- don't get
          high on your own supply.

The girl friend has departed and Elvira turns
her attention back to them, bored.

                    LOPEZ
          That's right. Course not
          everybody follows the rules.
          (eyeing Elvira)

                    HEAD WAITER
          There you go, Mr. Lopez.

He's popped the champagne cork and pours Dom
Perignon for Lopez.

                    LOPEZ
          (sipping)
          This the '64?

Head Waiter nods.

                    LOPEZ
          Give it to everybody and bring
          another, willya Jack?
          (to Tony)
          Five hundred fifty dollars for
          this bottle Tony, what do you
          think of that, hunh? For a
          bunch of fucking grapes --
          isn't that something?

                    ELVIA
          (to Tony)
          In France, it cost $100 but
          don't tell anybody in Miami.

Tony catches her eye. She looks away,
interested.

57     INT. BABYLON CLUB - NIGHT

A Man passes the table. Lopez calls out.

                    LOPEZ
          Hey, George -- buddy.

                    MAN
          Hey, Frank... how's the case
          coming?

The Man's eyes thread the table. He looks
sharp, heavy lidded, cigarette-eyed, his voice
a hoarse croak, a cigarette dangling from his
mouth, his manner cool but amicable with
Lopez. This is George Sheffield, Miami lawyer.

                    LOPEZ
          Oy, I shoulda come to you
          'stead of that putz, Neufeld.

                    SHEFFIELD
          Jack's a good lawyer. I taught
          him everything he knows.

                    LOPEZ
          Yeah, almost everything.

                    SHEFFIELD
          (to Elvira)
          Elvira, you look terrific...
          (to all)
          Enjoy yourselves.

He ambles off.

                    LOPEZ
          ...best goddamn lawyer in
          Miami. Cost a brick to pick up
          a phone.

Tony looking off at him, remembering it.

                    LOPEZ
          (raising his champagne glass)
          so... here's to old friends...
          and new friends.

They toast, Tony tasting it like it was Holy
Water.

                    LOPEZ
          Well, Tony?

                    TONY
          Hey, yeah, you're not kidding,
          this is good stuff, Frank.

Lopez laughs, likes the kid, tweaks him on the
cheek.

                    LOPEZ
          (checking Tony's threads)
          Yeah, get you some new
          clothes, some $500 suits,
          you'll look real sharp. I'd
          like you and your boys to
          handle some stuff for me,
          Tony, work with Omar here.
          We're doing something big next
          month. Running a string of
          mules out of Columbia. You do
          good on that, there'll be
          other things.

Omar doesn't like it but glances away.

                    TONY
          Hey, that sounds like fun,
          Frank. Thanks.

The music shifts to slow dancing.

                    ELVIRA
          (waving away cigar smoke)
          So, you want to dance, Frank
          or you want to sit here and
          have a heart attack?

                    LOPEZ
          Me Dance? I'd rather have a
          heart attack.

                    ELVIRA
          (rising)
          Don't foam into the Dom
          Perignon.

Glancing at Omar, sitting there obediently.
Her eyes say forget it.

                         ELVIRA
                    (to Tony)
                    How about you?


          Tony nods sure, looks at his boss.

                         LOPEZ
                    (waves)
                    Go on!


          They go.


58    INT. BABYLON CLUB - NIGHT

          It's interesting to watch Tony walk to the
          floor, leading Elvira. It's not so much an act
          of walking as it is an act of war, a tank
          bouncing anything or anybody off that gets in
          the way. Be just proceeds in a straight dead
          line, eyes forward. It's not that he doesn't
          see the people he bumps off, it's that he
          couldn't care less.

                         LOPEZ
                    (to Omar)
                    What do you think?

                         OMAR
                    I think he's a fucking
                    peasant.

                         LOPEZ
                    Yeah -- but you get guys like
                    that on your side, they break
                    their backs for you.


     CUT TO


59    INT. BABYLON CLUB DANCE FLOOR - NIGHT

          Tony and Elvira are dancing semiclose to a

slow Billy Joel dance tune. He's no great
shakes as a dancer, leaden in the legs and
shoulders.

                    TONY
          ...so what's your name, Elvira
          what?

                    ELVIRA
          St. James.

                    TONY
          Elvira St. James. Sounds like
          a nun or something. So where
          you from?

He bumps into an elderly couple dancing,
ignores them.

                    ELVIRA
          Baltimore...

                    TONY
          Baltimore? Where's that?

                    ELVIRA
          Look, it doesn't really matter.
          I'm getting a headache.

                    TONY
          Just trying to be friendly.

                    ELVIRA
          I've got enough friends --
          and I don't need another one,
          'specially one who just got
          off the banana boat.

He makes a point of looking at her.

                    TONY
          Hey, I didn't come over on no
          banana boat. I'm a political
          refugee here.

                    ELVIRA
          Oh, part of the Cuban crime
          wave?

Tony, pissed, bangs once more into the
elderly couple.

The man stops dancing, looks at him
exasperated but Tony doesn't see.

                    TONY
          Whatta you talking crazy for,
          whatsa matter with you?

                    ELVIRA
          (interrupting)
          I'm sorry. I didn't know you
          were so sensitive about your
          diplomatic status.

                    TONY
          ...Why you got this beef
          against the world? You got a
          nice face, you got great legs,
          you got the fancy clothes and
          you got this look in your eyes
          like you haven't been fucked
          good in a year. What's the
          problem, baby?

Elvira laughs at him, furious.

                    ELVIRA
          You know you're even stupider
          than you look. Let me give you
          a crash course, Jose whatever

your name is, so you know what
you're doing around here.

                    TONY
          (interrupting)
          Now you're talking to me, baby!

                    ELVIRA
          First who, where, why and
          how I fuck is none of your
          business, second don't call me
          'baby,' I'm not your baby and
          last, even if I was blind,
          desperate, starved and begging
          for it on a desert island,
          you'd be the last thing I'd
          ever fuck. You got the picture
          now -- so fuck off.

                    TONY
          Hey, thataway.

     She whips off the floor, pissed. He watches
     her, amused.

          CUT TO

60 thru 62 OMITTED

63     INT. CAR-DAWN

          Tony and Manny drive home in the broken
          down Monte Carlo sedan through the streets
          of Little Havana.

          They've been partying all night, clothes
          rumpled, Tony smoking his cigar, feeling good.

                    TONY
          That chick he's with... she
          loves me.

                    MANNY
              (driving)
          Oh yeah, how you know that?

                    TONY
          The eyes, Manny -- they don't
          lie.

                    MANNY
          You're serious? Tony, that's
          Lopez'S lady. He'll kill us.

                    TONY
          What are you kidding -- he's
          soft. I seen it in his face --
          booze and a cuncha tells him
          what to do.
     Pause.


63-A and 64 OMITTED

              CUT TO


65   EXT. TONY'S MOTHER'S HOUSE - SOUTHWEST MIAMI -
     LATE DAY

          The house, bathed by a torpid setting sun
          amicable to lizards and Spanish moss, sits
          undistinguished and without shielding trees in
          the midst of a lower middle class neighborhood
          with look-alike yards and streets without
          people.


66   INT. TONY'S CAR - SIMULTANEOUS DAY

          From his battered Monte Carlo across the curb,
          Tony, spruced up and nervous in a new suit,
          gets out carrying a bag of gifts. Manny is at
          the wheel, curious.

                              TONY
                  Be back in an hour okay.


67     EXT. DOWNTOWN MIAMI - SUNNY DAY - TWO MONTHS LATER


       The new Miami is rising ubiquitously-above
       Biscayne Bay, the camera moving past blossoming
       Skyscrapers, workmen, huge cranes, glass,
       mirrors booming upwards into a beautiful
       blue Florida sky, fleeced with perfectly white
       clouds... past a giant billboard:---


           HOW ABOUT A MILLION DOLLAR LOAN?
                  COME TALK TO US...
               AT THE BANCO DE MIAMI...
                       TODAY!


       Past banks of glass (Caribank, Ranco de
       Venezuela, Amerifirst)


       Insert a car sticker going by with the image
       of the American flag and the reminder: "Will
       the last American leaving Miami please bring
       the flag?"


       Tony and Manny, on a shopping spree, bop
       along an incredibly luxurious shopping mall
       lined with the latest stores, fashions,
       escalators, music, tropical plants, etc --
       a warm womb-like plastic heaven.


                              TONY
                  ...I shoulda been here 10 years
                  ago man. This town's like a
                  fig pussy dyin' to get fucked.
                  Paradise, man, paradise! I
                  coulda been a millionaire now.
                  Get my own golf course, a boat...


                              MANNY
                  I want a line of bluejeans


                                                          75

with my name on the chicks'
asses.

                    TONY
          ...yeah we gotta make some
          moves on our own Manny, we
          never gonna score the Big
          Money working for Frank.

                    MANNY
          Frank's okay.

                    TONY
          Yeah -- cause he buys you a
          suit? You thinkin' like a
          chickenhead again.

                    MANNY
          Frank's got an organization...

                    TONY
          Organization? I got more
          brains than Omar and he's
          bigger than me. That's not
          an organization. That's a
          disorganization. What do you do
          for a brain man? Piss in it?

                    MANNY
          Fuck you, somebody oughta
          shoot you, put you outta your
          misery.
          (seeing something)
          Hey, catch this tomato.

Catching the eye of one of two young Girls
passing, Manny primps for them.

                    MANNY
          Ooooh baby doll *(SEE NOTES)

                         TONY
          Yeah, what do you girls say?
          You wanna have some ice cream
          with us somewhere?

They glance at Tony and Nanny and hurry on.

Tony waves her off, then changes his mind and
runs up behind her and throws up her skirt and
peeks at her ass. Before she can react, he
hops away laughing as the two Cuban girls
ad-lib Spanish expletives at him.

                         MANNY
          Hey that's not cool, man. You
          wanna score one of these
          chicks, watch me. Mira!

He wiggles his tongue up and down, fast like a
small whirring motor part, then slips it back
into his mouth in the flick of an eye.

                         TONY
          ...the fuck was that?

                         MANNY
          You didn't see it? You weren't
          looking. Hey you gotta watch
          for it.

Does it again, quickly; it looks like a baby
robin's head peeking out of a nest in his
teeth, then it's gone.

                         TONY
          What the hell's that
          for -- eating bugs? That's
          disgustin'.

                         MANNY
          You think so hunh? Well you

                    don't know shit 'bout chicks
                    chico. When they see this,
                    they know. They go crazy.
                    They don't resist me.

          Does it again. Tony tries but lacks the speed
          and agility, provoking Manny's laughter. Manny
          double checks himself in a shop window.

                              MANNY
                    (doing it again)
                    Takes practice, mi sengre, but
                    they just love it when you
                    flop that pussy with it...

                              TONY
               Oooh... como! How 'bout that one?

          Pointing to a tall, cool blonde across the
          avenue.

                              MANNY
                    No problem.


67        EXT.. MIAMI SHOPPING STREET - DAY.

               Tony walks right out into the avenue, sticking
               out his arm and stopping traffic. Cars honk
               angrily but he couldn't give a shit.

                              TONY
                    Come on!

Manny follows as Tony now moves across the opposite lane,
a car screeching to a halt in front of him.

                              TONY
                    (points)
                    Okay Robert Redford, strut
                    your stuff.

The blonde has paused to look in a shop
window.

Manny stops alongside, pretends to look. When
he catches her eyes, he flicks his tongue.

She looks at him, confused, then back into the
window.

Manny looks back at Tony, winks, sidles closer
to her.

Tony, exiting off to the side, catches the
gaze of a somber child, four, toddling along
with it's mom. He makes his own version of a
funny face at the kid who looked back at him
puzzled. Tony produces another face. The kid
now smiles. The mother looks over. Tony
shrugs. She smiles and moves along.

Meanwhile, Manny has moved close to the blonde
and suggests something, his eyebrows raising,
the smile crooked. It takes a moment, then the
blonde smacks him across the face and walks
away.

Tony walks up to him, mocking.

                    TONY
          I'm telling you man you got it
          all mixed up. This country
          first you gotta get the money;
          then you get the power, and
          when you got the power, then
          you get the women -- then,
          chico, you got the world by
          the balls. Por Los cojones.

                    MANNY
          Hey Tony, last time this year
          you was in a fuckin' cage in

Cuba. Why don't you take it
easy chico, slow down, one
step at a time, be happy what
you got you know? You get on
your death bed you look around
you think to yourself "when
was I ever happy?"

Camera moving with Tony as he glances in an
elegant window displaying jewelry.

                TONY
        You be happy. I want what's
        comin' to me when I'm alive
        not when I'm dead.

                MANNY
        (shakes his head)
        Yeah, what's comin' to you
        Tony?

                TONY
        The world man and everything
        in it!

As he goes into the store, the camera panning
to the diamonds in the window.

CUT TO

65      EXT... TONY'S MOTHER'S HOUSE - SOUTHWEST MIAMI -
and     NIGHT
66

                MANNY
        Okay... be    cool.

Tony approaches the house, with the paper bag
held high against his chest.

67    EXT./INT. TONY'S MOTHER'S HOUSE - LATE DAY

> Tony's Mother opens the door. A stout aging woman with a powerful face, she's shook to her roots.

>               TONY
>         (gently, in Spanish)
>     Mami... long time...

>               MAMI
>     No postcards from jail, hunh?

> Pause.

> He doesn't offer to kiss her nor she him. Mother looks behind her. Someone else is in the house. Mother looks back as if she has no choice. She opens the door. He steps in. He looks.

68    INT. TONY'S MOTHER'S LIVING ROOM - NIGHT

> The interior is comprised of small, narrow rooms filled with religious objects from macumba and waist-high black Jesus statues in various corners. The floor is without rugs and mosaicked with inexpensive, Aztec-type tiles, the impression clean, cluttered, Catholic, somewhat depressing.

> Stepping forward to the center of the living room like a cautious cat is his nineteen-year-old sister Gina. Their eyes lock.

>               TONY
>         (moved)
>     Hi Gina...

>               GINA
>     Tony?

She looks at her mother confused. She's a naturally dark, curly-headed beauty with a slim, graceful figure and large-lidded eyes brimming with the same energy as Tony's. (She might also be recognizable from the snapshot we saw in Tony's possession.)

> TONY
> (covering his unwanted
> emotion)
> Yeah, look at you, you're
> beautiful... what's it been
> seven years? Last time I saw
> you, you looked like a boy.
> Now look at you, you got great
> big eyes just like me!  Yeah,
> so...

He holds out a wrapped gift towards her, about to give it.

> TONY
> I got this for you, no big
> deal but...

> GINA
> Oh Tony!

Gina suddenly explodes across the room and rushes into his arms grasping him fiercely.

> GINA
> ...it's you!

Tony, over her shoulder, catches his mother's eyes boring into him stonily.

> GINA
> I never thought I'd see you
> again -- never!

Tony, over her shoulder, opens the gift.

                    TONY
          Hey pussycat, c'mon -- you
          think they can keep a guy like
          me down?

Disengaging gently, he holds up the contents
of the gift box in font of her. It's a
beautiful diamond locket to wear around her
neck. Her eyes open wide.

                    TONY
          ...yeah for you... and look --
          here. What I got written on
          it...

     "To Gina From Tony. Always."

                    GINA
          It's beautiful Tony, it's just
          beautiful...

The mother is amazed at the cost of the gift.
Tony pulls out another present, for her.

                    TONY
          ...for you too Mama, look...

Moving towards her, he opens the package and
pulls out an exquisite pearl necklace. She
stares at it, doesn't take it. Gina comes
over, takes it for her.

                    GINA
          Mama, it's beautiful...
          (offers it, an unspoken, 'why
          don't you take it?')

Mama doesn't. Gina puts it away with her own.

                    TONY
          (holding Gina by the shoulder,
          making light of it)
          Well anyway, here we are hunh?
          The three musketeers! We made
          it to America hunh? Let's
          toast!

     Tossing the empty package aside, he pulls the
     last gift -- a bottle of champagne.

                    TONY
          Oye! To America!
          (singing)
          'America. America...'

CUT TO

69   INT. TONY'S MOTHER'S KITCHEN - NIGHT

     Mama, with things on her mind, is silently
     cooking a lunch, as Tony and Gina finish the
     champagne at the kitchen table.

                    GINA
          ...So Mama's still at the
          factory and I'm working
          part-time at a beauty parlor.
          I'm doing hair. Remember Hiram
          Gonzalez? His father had the
          barbershop?

     Tony nods.

                    GINA
          It's his place. Plus I'm going
          to junior college -- Miami
          Dade -- and in two more years
          I get my cosmetology license
          and then I'll be making
          enough...

                    TONY
          Yeah, well surprise, all
          that's over with starting
          today. I didn't bring up my
          kid sister to work in no
          hair shop...

Mama looks over at him on the words "bring up"
and he catches her look.

                    TONY
          ...and Mama don't have to sew
          in no factory.

He pulls out a bundle of cash, fifties and
hundreds, and starts peeling them off on the
table. Mama stops working, looks.

                    TONY
          (to Mama as he counts)
          Yeah, your son's made it Mama,
          he's a success. I wanted to
          surprise you. That's how come
          I didn't show my face around
          before. I wanted you to see
          what a good boy I been.

Pushes a thousand dollar stack towards her.

                    TONY
          That's a thousand dollars
          right there, Mama -- for you.

She approaches it cautiously, her fingers
riffling the bills, then looks back at
her son.

                    MAMA
          Who'd you kill for this Tony?

                    GINA
          (aghast)
          Mama!

                    TONY
          I didn't kill nobody Mama,
          (lying)

                    MAMA
          No? What are you doing now --
          banks or is it still bodegas,
          you and the others?

                    TONY
          C'mon Mama. Things are
          different. I'm working with
          this anti-Castro group. I'm an
          organizer now, we get a lotta
          political contributions...

                    MAMA
          Sure you do Tony -- with a gun
          sticking in somebody's face.
          All we read about in the
          papers is the animals like you
          and the killings, what about
          the Cubans who come here and
          work hard and make a good name
          for themselves? What about...

                    GINA
          (springing to her feet)
          What are you saying Mama! He's
          your son!

                    MAMA
          Son? I wish I had one. He's a
          bum! He was a bum then and
          he's a bum now!
          (to Tony, she's worked up like
          a madwoman now)

Who do you think you are, we
haven't heard a word from you
in five years and you suddenly
show up here and throw some
money around and you think you
can get my respect? You think
you can buy me with jewelry?
You think you can come into my
house with your hotshot
clothes and your gutter
manners and make fun of...

                    TONY
Hey Mama, come on, you don't
know what you're talking
about...

                    MAMA
No, no, that's not the way I
am Tony and that's not the way
I --
(emphasizing it)
I raised Gina to be. You're
not going to destroy her. I
don't need your money, thanks.
I work for my living -- and I
don't want you in this house
anymore and I don't want you
around Gina. So leave us
alone... go on, get out! And
take this lousy money with
you, it stinks!

She casts the bundle of bills back across the
table at him like dead lettuce.

A silence. Tony sits there livid, soothing
his scar, about to explode, but doesn't. Gina
mutters something in the silence.

                              GINA
                    Oh Mama... why do you got to
                    spoil it for everybody.
                    (to Tony)
                    I'm sorry Tony, I...


          Tony nods his head at his mother.

                              TONY
                    (gently)
                    Okay, Mama, okay...


     CUT TO


70       EXT. TONY'S MOTHERS HOUSE - NIGHT

          Tony walks out icily.

                              MANNY
                    (waiting in the car, seeing
                    his expression)
                    Relatives, hunh? A pain in the
                    ass, they ---

                              TONY
                    Shaddup!


          He's climbing into the car when Gina hurries
          out the house.

                              GINA
                    Tony!

                              MANNY
                    Hey who's that?


          Checks himself in the rearview mirror,
          slicks his hair. Tony and Gina talk next to
          the car.

                    GINA

     Tony... Mama -- since Papa
     took off.


                    TONY

     Hey forget Papa, we never had
     one, okay? He was a bum!


                    GINA

     (continuing)
     ...she's got a lot of hate in
     her Tony, she's proud, you got
     to understand that?


                    TONY

     (making light of it now)
     Hey it's okay, it's Mama, what
     do you want, she's Old World.


                    GINA

     Tony, I know you did some bad
     things back then. The Army, I
     know you got into some trouble.


                    TONY

     Communists you know, they're
     always trying to tell you what
     to do.


                    GINA

     Mama, she doesn't
     understand... but I just
     want you to know, y'know, I
     don't care. Five years, ten
     years, it doesn't matter how
     long you been away, you're
     my blood. Always.


     Pause. She stares intently at him,
     emphasizing it.

                    TONY
          Hey I know... I know.


She gives him a soft kiss. He takes out his
money roll.

                    TONY
          Say, I want you to keep this
          for yourself. Okay? Help Mama
          out, but don't tell her I gave
          you this, okay?


She hesitates... He nudges her on the cheek
and slaps the whole wad into her palm.

                    TONY
          Go on! Go out and have some
          fun, what the hell? You gonna
          beat yourself to death at
          nineteen, pussycat like you?


He gets in the car. She peers in.

                    GINA
          You can come by the shop y'know,
          any afternoon, I'll be there okay?


Her eyes fall on Manny at the wheel.

He smiles back with charm.

Gina's eyes pause on him, then withdraw. The
sedan drives.

71    INT. TONY'S SEDAN - NIGHT - MOMENTS LATER

                    MANNY
          (driving)
          Hey, cono, you never told me
          you had such a good-looking
          doll for a sister!

Tony looks at him icily.

                    TONY
          Stay away Manny, don't ever
          let me catch you fuckin'
          around with her, don't ever
          fuck around with her...

                    MANNY
          (feeling the heat)
          Sure... sure.

     A beat.


CUT TO


72   MONTAGE — PASSING TIME

          Music accompanying the flipping of calendar
          leaves.


73   U.S. CUSTOMS - MIAMI INTERNATIONAL AIRPORT- DAY

          Tony, spruce in his new three-piece suit with
          the diamond on the finger and the expensive
          watch, looks like the young ethnic American
          businessman in import-export as he steps in
          front of a chunky, young Customs Officer, who
          looks at him coldly.

                    CUSTOMS OFFICER
               Mind opening that, sir?

          Tony, calm, unzips the chic leather single
          suitcase, his eyes drifting around...

          A woman, with a child and toy panda in a baby
          carriage, is cursorily checked through an
          adjacent line.

A nun is waived through the third line.

A stockbroker waiting in a fourth line, glances nervously in Tony's direction.

Tony looks away, back at the Officer who is thoroughly ransacking the suitcase looking for a false bottom. He waits, confident.

An old man is waived through a fifth line.

74     OMITTED

75     EXT. DOLLY STASH'S HOUSE - MIAMI - DAY

The mother-type unscrews the handles of the baby carriage, pulling out the wrapped cocaine, while Chi-Chi extricates another load from the kid's panda bear which is now in shreds.

76     THE OLD MAN

Helped by Rafi, is removing a sophisticated false bottom from his suitcase, laminated and difficult to detect.

77     MANNY AND GASPAR

break open wooden clothes hangers concealing cocaine as the stockbroker changes clothes.

78     THE MOTHER

picks up the baby and removes cocaine from its diaper.

While:

79     THE FORMER NUN

in partial habit, steps out of the toilet, adjusting her underpants; she places a package of cocaine on a table, on which we now see approximately five kilos stacked.

80    TONY

counting out the cash for his mules, Omar there, over-looking the operation.

81    MIAMI INTERNATIONAL AIRPORT - DAY

Again. But this time going out.

The nun, now a housewife, going through an exit gate carrying hand luggage.

82    TONY

watching, glances up at the electronic information board — Houston clocks out the time and the boarding gate... we move to Los Angeles -- "on time" ---

Tony's eyes moving to the mother, now without the child, buying her ticket at the counters.

Manny joins him, nodding okay. Tony, with a glance at his watch, starts out the terminal. The roar of the aircraft blending with city sounds as we continue the rapid pace of the montage with music.

83    thru 85 OMITTED

86    EXT. GOLF COURSE - MIAMI - DAY

Frank Lopez has Tony and Chi-Chi out on the golf course. Tony never played before and gets frustrated, swings his club at the ball like a baseball bat -- Lopez getting a kick out of him. Chi-Chi naturally makes a perfect putt, shrugging when Tony looks over at him amazed.

87    INT. LAUNDRY RESTAURANT - NIGHT

The plush millionaire's restaurant is to be seen again. Frank has his arm around Tony, introducing him to a business-type. Elvira looks on.

88    INT. HIGH-FASHION STORE - DAY

In a high-fashion store, Tony buys a beautiful dress for Gina who is delighted when she sees herself in the mirror, hugs Tony. Manny watches, unable to take his eyes off her.

                    SALESLADY
            (admiringly to Tony)
            Your wife looks terrific in
            that.

                    TONY
            My wife? You gotta be kidding.

89 and 90    INT. LOBBY - LOPEZ CONDO - DAY

Elvira steps out of the lobby into the driveway. Tony is waiting for her. She's surprised.

                    TONY
            He got held up at the golf
            club. He told me to pick you
            up. He'll meet us at the race
            track.

Elvira contemplating him with distaste.

                              TONY
                    He said if he was late to bet
                    Ice Cream in the first. She
                    sighs, walks across the lobby.
                    He follows.

She steps out in a Gucci summer dress, looks
around. He points.

                              TONY
                    Over there...

She looks. The car is a yellow Cadillac
convertible with big fins and Snoopy the dwarf
dashboard statue with stickers all over the
fenders. Adding to the impression are Manny
and Chi-Chi waiting in the backseat.

                              ELVIRA
                    (registers it with distaste)
                    That thing? You must be
                    kidding.

                              TONY
                    (hurt)
                    Whaddaya mean, that's a
                    Cadillac.

                              ELVIRA
                    I wouldn't be caught dead in
                    that thing.

                              TONY
                    It's got a few years on it but
                    it's 'a creampuff.'

                              ELVIRA
                    It looks like somebody's
                    nightmare.

91    INT. LUXURY MOTOR SALES - CORAL GABLES - DAY

Camera moves around a slick, red Jaguar -- XG 6 -- with Tony, accompanied by Manny, Chi-Chi, the Salesman. Elvira waits aloofly off to the side.

                    TONY
          (to Elvira)
          So you like this better?

                    ELVIRA
          (shrugs)
          It's got style.

                    TONY
          Yeah it looks like one of them
          tigers from India.

                    MANNY
          (to Elvira)
          Tony been dragging me around
          to the zoos, looking at
          tigers. He wants to buy one of
          them too.
          (amused)
          He do that he gonna have no
          friends left. Not that he got
          any now.

                    TONY
          You'll like the tiger Manny,
          you'll see.

                    ELVIRA
          You going to drive around with
          a tiger in your passenger seat
          Tony?

                    TONY
          Yeah... maybe some lady tiger
          (to Salesman)
          How much?

                    SALESMAN
          Twenty-eight thousand dollars.
          Fully equipped.

                    TONY
          (genuinely)
          That all?

                    SALESMAN
          Machine gun turrets are extra.

                    TONY
          (circling the car)
          Funny guy hunh... Manny,
          c'mere.

Manny comes over and Tony walks him along the
car, in quieter tones.

                    TONY
          Get these sections bullet-
          proofed... here... here...
          these windows...

                    MANNY
          Yeah.

                    TONY
          ...and a phone with a
          scrambler.

                    MANNY
          ...okay.

                    TONY
          ...And one of those radio
          scanners, y'know, pick out
          flying saucers and stuff.

                    MANNY
          Yeah a good one.

                    ELVIRA
          (joining them)
          Don't forget the fog lights.

                    TONY
          Yeah in case I go to the
          swamps, good idea.

                    ELVIRA
          (impatiently)
          I thought you were taking me
          to Frank?

                    TONY
          (glances at his watch)
          We still got an hour. You
          hungry?

                    ELVIRA
          No but I'm bored.

                    TONY
          Figgers. Check it out, will
          you Manny and pay the guy and
          grab a taxi out to the
          track...

                    MANNY
          Thanks, yeah...

                    TONY
          (before leaving)
          Oh yeah...

He reaches into his pocket, pulls out a decal,
a private joke. He slaps it on the rear
fender. It's the same sticker we saw earlier
of the American flag with the epitaph, "Will
the Last American leaving Miami please bring
the flag?"

Elvira wonders about it as he joins her.

                    TONY
          Somebody gotta keep the
          animals out.

92    EXT. LUXURY MOTORS - DAY

          Tony leads her to his yellow Cadillac
          convertible parked out of eyesight of the others.

                    TONY
          I'm glad you came. I wouldn't
          buy the car you didn't like it.

                    ELVIRA
          Planning on driving the girls
          crazy, aren't you?

                    TONY
          Yeah — you know who.

          They get in the car.

                    ELVIRA
          And what would Frank say?

          She has a coke vial out, casually hits one
          nostril, then other, then takes a last hit
          through the mouth.

                    TONY
          I like Frank but I like you
          better.

          He reaches over and takes the coke from her.
          Does a toot, staring at her. She's uncomfortable.
          When he finishes he makes as if to return it
          to her. She leans to take it. He kisses her.
          She goes with it.

Pause. She pulls back.

                    ELVIRA
          (same tone of voice as before)
          Don't get confused, Tony. I
          don't fuck around with the
          help.

As he puts the key into the ignition, Tony has
this wolfish grin on his face.

CUT TO

93    INT. COCAINE LAB - BOLIVIA - DAY

Subtitle appears:

                    COCHABAMBA, BOLIVA

Alejandro Sosa is a playboy, about six-foot-
two, black wavy hair, athletic body and a
Copacabana tan, the clothes, a casual polo
shirt and the latest pants from Calvin Klein.

On his wrist is a flashy gold ID bracelet with
"Alex" written in diamonds and on the other
wrist a gold Rolex with a bezel full of
diamonds worth maybe $30,000. His eyes fizzle
with an energy derived not from drugs but the
continual excitement of his toys and his
money.

Accompanying him everywhere is the Shadow, a
thin, intense venomous-looking Hispanic man in
his thirties, he has the look of death in an
unsmiling face. He is always in proximity to
his Jefe, usually slightly behind the person
or persons addressing Sosa -- in a sort of
garotte position, his eyes swivelling to stare
down the person who might glance at him. He is
a continual source of tension underplaying the

scenes, particularly coming to affect Omar who
is insecure to begin with.

Sosa is showing Tony and Omar through his coke
processing lab, past four coal-fired stoves,
each with massive iron kettles bubbling with
coca paste... across to a row of ovens where
the refined coke dries. The chemists and
Indians working there all acknowledge "Del
rey del rey" as he passes, as proud of his
factory as a vine grower his vineyard.

                    SOSA
          ...so this and my other factory
          I can guarantee production of
          200 kilos refined every month
          of the year. Problem is I have
          no steady market. Some months
          I can't get rid of fifty keys,
          other months I have to do 2 to
          300 keys, it's crazy, hunh?
          Nobody can run a business that
          way ---


                    OMAR
          I know what you mean Mr. Sosa,
          we got the same problems up in
          Miami, the demand varies for
          us too, month to month...

Sosa looks at him like that's obvious and
moves on. In his skinny suit, with the wet
cigarette clamped between his nervous fingers,
Omar's not quite in his league with Sosa.

Tony, awed by the scope of it all, follows
along, stops to look at a sample of the dried
coke. The Shadow stops, eyeballs him.

Tony eyeballs him back, playing a game with
him, then samples the coke off his thumb into

his nose. Pause. His expression says I like
it. He moves on.

The Shadow moves with him.

>                    SOSA
>           (meanwhile)
>           ...Basically what I'm looking
>           for is somebody to share the
>           risks with me, somebody in the
>           States who might guarantee me
>           something like... say 150
>           kilos a month.

>                    OMAR
>           That's a big commitment Mr.
>           Sosa. It's too bad Frank's not
>           here. Something like that you
>           should talk to him.

>                    SOSA
>           Yes, it would've been nice if
>           he could have come.

>                    TONY
>           (cutting  in)
>           ...and he'd like meeting you
>           too Mr. Sosa. But with his
>           trial coming up y'know, it's
>           not so easy for him to slip
>           outta the country right now,
>           y'understand?

>                    SOSA
>           (taking the measure of Tony,
>           sarcastic)
>           So he sent you?

>                    TONY
>           Yeah, something like that. You
>           sure got good stuff in there

                    Mr. Sosa -- class A shit.

          Looking over the laboratory like it was his.
          Omar glances at him, annoyed.

                              SOSA
                    We'll talk at my house. Shall
                    we go...

94        INT. SOSA VILLA - BOLIVIA - DAY

          The camera moves past a spectacular view of
          the mountains to a cavernous dining room
          highlighted by huge paintings from the Spanish
          classical period and ornate candelabra. At the
          table are Sosa, Omar, Tony. The Shadow sits
          impassively in a folding chair off to the
          side, watching Omar and Tony. Tony is
          impressed, looking at the plates, the glasses,
          the silverware, uncomfortable, trying to fit
          in. He eats the salmon off a silver plate with
          oafish movements of his knife and fork as the
          servants move to and fro, constantly changing
          dishes, confusing Tony (ad-lib during scene).

                              SOSA
                    (to Omar)
                    ...say Lopez guarantees me 150
                    keys a month for a year, and
                    he picks it up down here, I
                    could sell it to him for as
                    little as 7000 a kilo. You
                    **cannot** do better than that.

                              OMAR
                    Well, we do that we gotta take
                    the risk of moving it. Also
                    we'd be cutting out the
                    Columbians. You know what that
                    means?

                    TONY
          That means we gotta go to war
          with `em.

Sosa looks over at him, not quite knowing yet
what to make of this guy.

                    SOSA
          When we cut out the Columbians
          we take risks -- on both
          sides.

                    TONY
          Split the risk. Guarantee your
          delivery as far as Panama.

                    SOSA
          Panama? Risky? It costs me
          more. There I'd sell maybe
          13.5 a key.

                    TONY
          13.5! What are you nuts? We
          still gotta take the shit to
          Florida. You know what that's
          like these days? They got the
          Navy all over the fuckin'
          place. They got frogmen,
          they got EC2s with satellite
          tracking shit in 'em, they
          got fuckin' Bell 209 assault
          choppers up the ass, we're
          losing one out of every nine
          loads. It's no duck walk for
          us anymore, y'know. Forget it.

Omar is looking at him, ready to explode at
his blithe assumption of power -- whereas Sosa
chuckles, amused by his brashness, starting to
be intrigued by this animal.

                         SOSA
          What do you suggest is a
          fair...? Excuse me.


Interrupted, Sosa looks over at his black aide
who suddenly appears at the door, apparently
with a message. Sosa waves him in.

The black aide - The Skull -- is a slim,
tall imposing man with academic, horn-rimmed
glasses and close-cropped hair on a huge and
impressive skull. He combines the physical
qualities of an animal with an intellectual.
As he approaches, he glances down the table,
his eyes falling briefly on Omar who doesn't
connect. The Skull falters -- just for a
moment -- then continues towards Sosa with
the same stony, loyal expression.

Sosa lends his ear and the Skull whispers his
information.

A beat. He whispers a second thought. Sosa
reacts minimally. Then he nods, dismissing the
Skull who heads out the room. Sosa glances at
his gold Rolex.


                         OMAR
          (meanwhile to Tony in a whisper)
          Shaddup willya Montana, I'm
          doing the talking here!

Tony shrugs.

                         SOSA
          Where were we?


                         TONY
          Panama. You're looking for a
          partner, right?

Omar shoots a poisonous glance at Tony.

                    SOSA
          ...something like that.
           (chuckles)

                    OMAR
          Look Mr. Sosa, we're getting
          ahead of ourselves here. I'm
          down on Frank's authority to
          buy 200 keys, that's it,
          that's my limit. I got no
          right to negotiate for Frank
          Lopez on anything larger than
          that. So why don't we...

                    TONY
          Hey Omar why don't you let
          the man finish, hunh? Let him
          propose his proposition.

                    OMAR
          Hey Montana, you got no
          authority here, okay! I
          started you in this
          business, all right,
          so shut the fuck up!

                    TONY
           (shrugs)
          Frank'll love it. Don't worry
          about it.

                    OMAR
          That's up to Frank -- not you.

He looks embarrassed at Sosa who has been
watching, sensing also an advantage in
the split.

                    OMAR
          I'm sorry about this, Mr.
          Sosa...

                    SOSA
          It's all right. Maybe your
          partner's right. Maybe you
          should talk to Frank.

                    OMAR
          (a beat)
          Okay. I don't think this is
          something I want to do on an
          overseas phone, but I can go
          back to Miami and talk to
          Frank personally.

                    SOSA
          (without hesitation)
          Good. My chopper can take
          you to Santa Cruz now. I
          have a jet there that'll
          have you in Miami in five
          hours. You can be back here
          tomorrow. For lunch.

          Omar is taken aback by the speed of the plan.

                    OMAR
          Yeah I guess so...

                    TONY
          Great.

                    SOSA
          (glancing at Tony, to Omar)
          ...leave your friend here.
          While you're gone maybe
          he can tell me how to run
          my business.

                    OMAR
            (doesn't like it)
            I don't think that...

                    TONY
            (lighting a cigar)
            Hey it's okay. You tell Frank
            I'm keeping this guy on ice
            for him...

       Sosa laughs. Omar scowls.

   CUT TO

95     EXT. SOSA VILLA - DAY

       The helicopter blades whirr. The Skull waits
       inside with the Shadow. They both stare at:

       Omar, who, with one hesitant look, steps
       inside.

       The chopper lifts off the lawn, the camera
       moving to the polo players exercising in the
       distance...a woman on a horse rides by and
       we swing with her towards the villa.

       Sosa walks Tony down an outside gallery
       towards the veranda where servants lay out
       the coffee and fruits.

                    TONY
            You know why they say Cubans
            are all screwed up?

                    SOSA
            Why?

                    TONY
            'Cause the island's in the
            Caribbean, the government's in

Russia, the Army's in Angola,
and the people live in Miami.

Sosa laughs. They reach the veranda, Tony
glancing past Sosa to an exotic-looking, dark-
eyed senorita who gets off her horse, held by
a servant, and joins them.

                    TONY
          (overlapping the joke)
          ...They got a beard there
          that's all. With a cigar and a
          big mouth.

                    SOSA
          Maybe he'll move to Miami
          too... Gabriella, my rose --
          how was the ride?

Sosa changes his personality completely with
her, dewy-eyed and loving. They peck each
other's cheek lightly.

                    GABRIELLA
          (distracted)
          Lovely... but the sheep in the
          north pasture, they're de-
          stroying the grass, it's turn-
          ing yellow. You must move them
          darling.

                    SOSA
          I'll take care of it myself.

                    GABRIELLA
          (turning to go)
          ...and don't forget we have
          the Rinaldi's at eight.

                    SOSA
          Of course not. Uh -- an

                    associate of mine. From Miami.
                    Tony Montana...
                    (to Tony)
                    My fiance, Gabriella Montini.

                              TONY
                    Hello...

She nods to him in that somewhat uninterested,
rude, upperclass Latin way.

                            GABRIELLA
                    It's a pleasure.

She withdraws. Tony watches her go.

                              TONY
                    I gotta hand it to you. You
                    got everything a man could
                    want.

Sosa, pleased, reaches for an expensive set
of binoculars on the patio table, looks up
through them, at the helicopter rising off
the lawn.

                              SOSA
                    (focusing the binoculars)
                    I like you Tony. There's no
                    lying in you... Unfortunately
                    I don't feel the same way
                    about the rest of your
                    organization.

Tony glances up at the chopper, the servant
pouring coffee for him.

                              TONY
                    Uh — Whaddaya getting at, Mr.
                    Sosa?

                    SOSA
          I mean Omar Suarez.


Tony, puzzled, glances up at the chopper which
now hovers there high above the estate.


Sosa passes him the binoculars.

                    SOSA
          This garbage was recognized by
          my associate at lunch. From
          several years ago. In New
          York. He was an informer for
          the police...


Tony, astonished, looks up.


96      THROUGH THE BINOCULARS - OMAR


          terrified, being positioned at the door of the
          chopper by the Shadow and the Skull, his hands
          tied to his back and a length of thick rope
          looped around his neck. He is struggling
          backwards in vain.

                    SOSA
          He put Vito Duval and the
          Ramos Brothers -- Nello and
          Gino — away for life. My
          associate used to work up
          there.


Through the binoculars — they throw Omar out
of the chopper and he flies downwards and
jerks back up as the rope stretches taut,
snapping his neck. He hangs there like a
broken doll on a string as the chopper moves
out of sight.


A silence.

shaken, lowers the binoculars. Sosa watches
him closely for his reaction. Tony looks back
at him, contemplative. Sosa goes over, pours
himself some coffee.

                    SOSA
          So how do I know you're not a
          'chivato' too Tony?

                    TONY
          (angry, stalks up to him)
          Hey Sosa -- get this straight
          right now! I never fucked
          anybody over in my life didn't
          have it comin' to him -- okay!
          All I got's my two balls -- my
          word -- and I don't break 'em.
          For nobody. That piece of shit
          up there I never liked, I
          never trusted. For all I know
          he's the guy who set me up and
          got my buddy Angel Fernandez
          killed. But that's history.
          I'm here. He's not. You wanna
          go on with me, say it. You
          don't, make your move,
          hodedor!

                    SOSA
          (moves away)
          I think you speak from the
          heart Montana, but I say to
          myself this Lopez -- your
          boss -- he has 'chivatos'
          like that working for him,
          his judgment stinks. So I
          think to myself, what other
          mistakes has this Lopez guy
          made, how can I trust his

                    organization... hunh? You tell
                    me Tony.

                              TONY
                    Hey Frank's smart. Don't blame
                    him for that animal. It's
                    crazy business we're in, it
                    can happen to anybody -- even
                    you y'know. I'll talk to Frank
                    myself. I'll fix this thing up
                    right between you.
                    (then)
                    You got my word on that.

          Sosa approaches Tony, focusing an intense
          stare on him, makes an elaborate gesture of
          putting his hands out, Tony following the
          pantomine, puts his out. Sosa now grips them.

                              SOSA
                    You speak with your eyes
                    muchacho. I think -- you
                    and I -- we can work this
                    thing out, do business a long
                    time together. Just remember --
                    it's the only thing I ever tell
                    you -- don't fuck me Tony,
                    don't ever try to fuck me.

          Their eyes locked together.

     CUT TO


98   AERIAL VIEW - MIAMI - TWILIGHT

                    In all its Caribbean splendor with the
                    long curving beach and rich white buildings,
                    bathed in a lovely violet light. Music theme
                    continuing over.

     REVERSE WIDE TO

99      EXT. LOPEZ MOTORS AUTO DEALERSHIP –
        LITTLE HAVANA – DAY

                In long shot we see an agitated Lopez entering
                his dealership with his bodyguard. Against a
                background of used American cars without great
                distinction, he ad-libs his way through some
                customers and salesmen, shaking hands and
                acting like everybody's favorite uncle...
                'till we see him approach Tony, who is waiting
                for him with Manny outside his office. He
                jerks his head. Inside. They go.

        CUT TO


100     INT. AUTO LOPEZ OFFICE – DAY

                The office is highly decorated with plaques,
                momentos, Cuban patriot flags, and lots of
                photographs, centering on JFK and RFK shaking
                the hand of Lopez who now stares incredulously
                at Tony.

                            LOPEZ
                    (livid)
                    You **what**! You made a deal
                    for fucking **eighteen million
                    dollars** without even checking
                    with me! What are you crazy
                    Montana, **are you crazy**!


                            TONY
                    Hey take it easy Frank, cono.


                            LOPEZ
                    Cono my ass!


                            TONY
                    At 10.5 a key, it's pure
                    Frank... we can't lose money,
                    no way, we make seventy-five

**million** on this deal, Frank.
Seventy-five mill! That's
serious money.

                    LOPEZ
          Yeah and what's Sosa gonna do
          to me when I don't come up
          with the first five million
          dollars on this deal -- send
          me a bill? He's gonna send hit
          squads up here that's what.
          There's gonna be war in the
          streets.

                    TONY
          Frank... Frank...

                    LOPEZ
             (ranting)
          You know what this fucking
          trial is costing me in legal
          fees, Montana? You expect me
          to believe Omar was a stoolie
          'cause Sosa said so? And you
          bought that line?
             (pause, eyeing Tony)
          Maybe I made a mistake sending
          you down there? Maybe you and
          Sosa know something I don't
          know?

                    TONY
          You saying I'm not being
          straight with you Frank?

Lopez's bodyguard shifts. Manny slips his hand
closer to his belt.

                    LOPEZ
             (carefully)
          Let's just say I want things

to stay the way they are. For
now. Stall your deal with
Sosa.

Long pause. Tony's eyes meeting Lopez's. He
gave Sosa his word.

                    TONY
          (finally)
          ...have it your way boss.

He turns to leave, nods to Manny.

                    LOPEZ
          Montana... just remember I am
          the boss.

                    TONY
          Sure you're the boss.

Gets to the door, Manny joining him.

                    LOPEZ
          Y'know I told you when you
          started Tony, the guys who
          last in this business are guys
          who fly straight, real low
          key, real quiet... the guys
          who want it all, the chicks
          and the champagne and the
          flash -- they don't last.

Tony, saying nothing, goes out the door with
Manny.

101   EXT. AUTO LOPEZ OFFICE

          Just outside the door, Tony glances at Manny's
          question-mark expression.

                              TONY
                         (with steel)
                         Fuck him!


          CUT TO


101-A     EXT. SHEFFIELD'S OFFICE BUILDING -
          ESTABLISHING SHOT - NIGHT

102       INT. LAWYER'S OFFICE — NIGHT

                    Tony, impeccable in Cardin whites, and Manny,
                    also slicked up, are shown by an elegant
                    secretary into a plush office. Behind the
                    desk sits the heavy-lidded, cigarette-eyed
                    lawyer, George Sheffield smoking yet another
                    cigarette, his voice a hoarse gravelled croak,
                    the eyes -- with their deadman stare --
                    always pausing before they speak. He doesn't
                    get up from his desk. His hair is flaming red.
                    We saw him before, at the Babylon Club.

                              SHEFFIELD
                    What can I do for you Montana?

                              TONY
                         (indicates Manny)
                    My partner. Manny Ray.

                    Manny, standing in the b.g., nods... Sheffield
                    shifts his eyes briefly, back to Tony who
                    plops himself in a chair.

                              TONY
                    So George, they tell me you're
                    the best lawyer in town.

                              SHEFFIELD
                    Did they also tell you how
                    expensive I am?

                    TONY
          Hey it's like J.P. Morgan says
          -- if you gotta ask, you're
          outta your league.

                    SHEFFIELD
          I see you been reading your
          American history Montana,
          what've you done lately to
          earn a place in it?

                    TONY
          (chuckles)
          I'm trying to stay outta it,
          y'know what I mean? I'm
          expanding my operation. So I
          want a class guy like you on
          the payroll -- advising me.
          Starting now.

                    SHEFFIELD
          (a longer pause than usual)
          ...Start with a $100,000.
          Cash. On the table.

                    TONY
          (an equal pause}
          Sure...

          He sticks out his hand. Manny slaps an
          envelope in it. Tony begins counting out
          the cash, right on the tabletop.

103    EXT. LOPEZ CONDO - SOUTH MIAMI - DAY

          Tony waits in his red Jaguar in the driveway
          of the building. Lopez and his bodyguard exit
          the building. A limousine pulls up. Tony
          watches. The threesome get in the limo and
          drive away. Tony gets out of the car, crosses
          to the entrance.

104    INT. LOPEZ CONDO - DAY

Tony waits outside the door, pushes the
buzzer again. Elvira opens it, a look of
utter surprise on her face. She's in jeans,
barefoot and casual.

                    ELVIRA
        Tony?

                    TONY
        Hi there.

Elvira looks at him, still astonished and
waiting for an explanation. There is none.

                    ELVIRA.
        Uh... you just missed Frank.

                    TONY
        I didn't come here to see
        Frank.

She looks at him amazed. The balls on this
guy!

                    ELVIRA
        (cooling to him fast)
        This is not the time or the
        place. Next time make an
        appointment first.

She tries to slam the door in his face but he
blocks it and bulls in.

                    TONY
        I got something important to
        tell ya. Why don't you make
        some drinks and act normal.

                    ELVIRA
          Sure. Why not? We're all
          normal here.

She heads for the pool, nonplussed. Tony
closes the door, eases slowly across the
room towards her, awkwardly trying to make
conversation.

                    TONY
          I heard you was in Europe
          traveling 'round all by
          yourself. Woman like you
          shouldn't have to travel
          alone...
          (pause, no response)
          I been traveling myself.

                    ELVIRA
          Broadening your intellect. I
          heard.

                    TONY
          What else d'you hear?

                    ELVIRA
          I heard you and Frank aren't
          working together anymore.

                    TONY
          Yeah. It makes things easier
          this way, don't it?

She's puzzled. He drinks a toast.

                    TONY
          Here's to the land of
          opportunity.

                    ELVIRA
          For you maybe.

She drinks to it.

> TONY
> Hey, do you like kids?

> ELVIRA
> Kids? Sure, why not -- as long
> as there's a nurse.

> TONY
> Good. 'Cause I like kids too.
> I like boys and girls.

She's waiting. He paws the ground, awkward as
a bull.

> ELVIRA
> That's broad of you, Tony.
> Travelling really helped.
> Look, Frank's going to be back
> any moment and when he walks
> through that...

> TONY
> Yeah. Yeah -- fuck Frank.
> Look, here's the story. I'm
> from the gutter but I climbed
> out of it. I'm not the
> smartest guy in the world but
> I got guts and I know the
> streets and I'm making the
> right connections. With the
> right woman, there's no
> stopping me. I could go to
> the top, I could be somebody
> here in Miami. I could be
> like Frank but bigger — The
> biggest!...

Elvira's looking at him like he's on the moon.

                    TONY
          Anyway what I came up here to
          tell you is that... uh I like
          you. I think you're terrific.
          I known this the first time I
          seen you. You belong to me.
          We're tigers. The two of us...
          I want you to marry me and be
          the mother of my children.

Silence.

                    ELVIRA
          (stunned)
          Me? Marry you?

She laughs, a short harsh laugh.

                    TONY
          (sincere)
          Yeah... marry me.

                    ELVIRA
          What about Frank? What are you
          going to do about Frank?

                    TONY
          Frank's not gonna last...
          (puts down the drink, puts his
          hand on hers)
          I'm not looking for an answer
          right now Elvira, but I want
          you to think about it, okay? I
          want you to think hard... I'll
          see you the next time.

He goes. She stares at him, still dazed, yet
deep down -- flattered.

83    INT. BABYLON CLUB - NIGHT

The place is raging tonight as Tony and Manny
arrive, in tuxedos, making their way through
the crowd greeting the many people who know
them now. We might note Tony has refined the
art of walking and no longer bulls people out
of his path, he angles through them.

                    OWNER
          (indicating a table)
          Over here.

Tony stops, spots his sister Gina, in an
expensive looking dress, with a flashy young
Cuban guy in a burgundy suit.

                    TONY
          What the fuck is she doing
          here, she's...
          (heading towards her)

                    MANNY
          (stops him)
          Hey c'mon Tony, it's okay,
          it's just a disco for
          chrissake. What do you
          give her money for if you
          don't want her to go out,
          have some fun?

Gina spots Tony, hesitates, waves to him.
Manny waves back. Tony nods. Burgundy suit
checks them out.

                    TONY
          Who's she with?

                    MANNY
          Some kid, he works for Luco,
          he's harmless...

Tony spots a Large Man coming towards him.
Caucasian, about 250 pounds.

                    TONY
          Keep your eye on her. Make
          sure he don't dance too close.

                    MANNY
          Sure Tony.

                    LARGE MAN
          (intersecting)
          Hello Tony, you remember me?

                    MANNY
          (drifting away)
          I'll be at the table.

                    TONY
          (to the Large Man)
          Yeah, sure. You're...
          (snaps fingers trying to
          remember)
          ...Bernstein, right. Mel
          Bernstein. Narcotics, right?

                    BERNSTEIN
          That's right, Tony. I think we
          better talk.
          (indicates a quieter area)

There's something ugly in his smile, maybe
it's 'cause just the eyes do the smiling.

                    TONY
          Talk about what, what's there
          to talk about? I ain't killed
          anybody lately.

                    BERNSTEIN
          No not lately but we can go

back to ancient history. Like
Emilio Rebenga, like a bunch
of whacked Indians at the
Sun-Ray Motel in Miami Beach...

                    TONY
          Oh yeah?... you know Mel
          whoever's giving you your
          information must be taking
          you guys for a long ride.

                    BERNSTEIN
          Are we gonna talk or am I
          gonna bust your wiseass
          spic balls, Tony baby --
          here and now?

Tony looks at him.

106    INT. BABYLON CLUB - CORNER TABLE - TONY AND MEL

       in a corner of the Babylon -- talking.

                    BERNSTEIN
          ...yeah, so the news on the
          street is you're bringing in a
          lot of yeyo Tony... that
          you're no longer a small-time
          hood, you're public property
          now, and the Supreme Court
          says your privacy can be
          invaded...

                    TONY
          No shit -- how much?

                    BERNSTEIN
          (doodling on a piece of paper)
          There's an answer to that
          too...

He holds the paper up briefly in front of
Tony. It says "25,000."

                    TONY
          (reacts)
          That's a big number.

                    BERNSTEIN
          That's on a monthly basis.
          Every month the same thing.
          You know how this works, don't
          you? We tell you who's moving
          against you, we shake down who
          you want shaken down, if you
          have a real problem in a
          collection, we'll step in for
          you. I got eight killers with
          badges working for me. When we
          hit, it hurts... Same thing
          works the other way. You feed
          me a bust now and then, some
          new cowboy wants to go into
          business you let us know --
          we like snacks, it looks good
          on the record.

                    TONY
          S'pose I give you the money,
          how do I know you're the last
          bull I gotta grease? What
          about Metro, Lauderdale,
          DEA -- how do I know what
          rock they're gonna come out
          from under?

                    BERNSTEIN
          That's none of our business,
          Tony, we don't cross no lines.
          (getting up)
          I don't want this discussion
          going farther than this

                    table. My guys have families,
                    they're legitimate cops, I
                    don't want none of 'em getting
                    embarrassed 'cause if my guys
                    are gonna suffer, then they're
                    gonna make you suffer.
                    Comprendre?... Oh yeah and I
                    got a vacation comin' up. I
                    wanna take the wife to London,
                    England. We never been there.
                    Throw in two round-trip
                    tickets. First class.

Tony just stares at him. Bernstein smiles,
points.

                         BERNSTEIN
                    I like the scar. Nice. Like
                    Capone. But you oughta smile
                    more, Tony. Enjoy yourself.
                    Everyday above ground's a good
                    day.

He winks and goes. Tony sits there brooding on
it, eyes flicking back to the dance floor.

Burgundy suit there is snuggling up to Gina on
the dance floor. Too close.

Tony is getting pissed, he looks around for
Manny, then spots...

107   INT. BABYLON CLUB ENTERANCE - NIGHT

        Elvira walking into the club, followed by
        Lopez and Ernie, the bodyguard. Lopez is
        delayed at the door by his buddy, the Owner,
        and Elvira drifts in. His attention diverted
        from Gina, Tony goes towards her. She sees
        him coming, glances in Frank's direction.
        Tony comes right up to her.

                         TONY
              Hi...


                         ELVIRA
              Hello, Tony.


         Lopez, in conversation with the Owner, glances
         over, sees Tony with Elvira, his expression
         narrows.

                         TONY
              So... did you think about what
              I said? About the kids?


                         ELVIRA
              Tony, you're really nuts you
              know -- you really are.


         Lopez comes over, takes Elvira's arm, and
         smiles at Tony.


                         LOPEZ
              Hey Tony, why don't you get
              your own girl?


                         TONY
              That's what I'm doing, Frank.


         Tense look on Frank's face. The bodyguard
         circles.


                         LOPEZ
              (without a smile)
              Then go do it somewhere else.
              Get lost.


                         ELVIRA
              Frank, he was only...


                         TONY
              (ignoring her)

                    Maybe I don't hear so good
                    sometimes, man.

                              LOPEZ
                    You won't be hearing anything,
                    you go on like this.

                              TONY
                    You gonna stop me?

Frank is livid.

                              LOPEZ
                    You're fucking right I am.
                    I'm giving you orders. Blow.
                    (Esfumate)

The bodyguard moves closer to Tony who
doesn't move.

Manny suddenly slides into frame, backing Tony.

                              TONY
                    (icy)
                    Orders? There's only one thing
                    that gives and gets orders,
                    cabron -- balls.

Pause. Something's about to pop, turns
back just at the crest. Lopez abruptly
turns away.

                              LOPEZ
                    (to Elvira)
                    Let's go!

                              ELVIRA
                    Frank, this is ridiculous...

                              LOPEZ
                    C'mon!

He crowds her. Angry, she goes. Tony watches as they exit the club.

                    MANNY
          What happened?

                    TONY
          That cocksucker! -- He put
          that homicide prick Bernstein
          on me.

They stroll back to the table.

                    MANNY
          What for?

                    TONY
          The Emilio Rebenga hit.
          Remember that.

                    MANNY
          You're kidding!

                    TONY
          Who else knew about it?
          Omar's fertilizer, ain't he?
          Lopez is letting me know he's
          got weight on me.

                    MANNY
          I don't know, things don't
          look so good here, Tony. Maybe
          we should get outta town for a
          while, y'know go up to New York?

                    TONY
          You go. I like the weather
          here just fine.

He stops, his eyes darting to pick out Gina
laughing as she follows burgundy suit out of the

main room and down the stairs to the toilets.
Without hesitation, his irritation peaking
now, Tony darts after her.

                    MANNY
          Hey, where you going?

He doesn't answer.

CUT TO

108     INT. BABYLON CLUB - STAIRS AND LADIES ROOM - NIGHT

          Tony comes down the plush velvet stairs,
          flings himself into the Ladies room... the
          ladies, surprised, look back at him. No Gina.

109     INT. BABYLON CLUB - MEN'S ROOM AND STAIRS — NIGHT

          He moves over to the Men's room, throws the
          door open. There are four legs visible in one
          of the stalls. Tony moves past two men washing
          up, and hurls himself against the door.

          It crashes open on Gina in the act of snorting
          coke, with burgundy suit running his hands
          along her ass.

                    GINA
               (shocked)
          Tony!

                    TONY
          What are you doing! What are
          you doing!

          He grabs burgundy suit by the collar and whips
          him several times into the wall.

                    GINA
               (trying to restrain him)

Tony! What're you doing!
You're crazy!

He rips the coke out of her hands and scatters
it across the tiles.

                    TONY
          (to Gina)
          What are you doing with this
          shit, hunh?
          (back to burgundy suit)
          Get the fuck out of here,
          maricon, y'hear, I'll kill
          you next time.

                    GINA
          Fernando!

                    TONY
          (to Gina)
          Shaddup!

Manny runs in, several others now looking in
from the hall.

                    MANNY
          Tony!

Tony shoves burgundy suit, out of the stall,
past Manny.

                    TONY
          Go on!

                    GINA
          What the hell is...

                    TONY
          You think it's cute somebody
          puttin' their hands all over

                    your ass, my kid sister, hunh?
                    In a toilet!

                              GINA
                    It's none of your business!

                              TONY
                    The fuck it isn't! Three
                    dollar hooker, that's what you
                    are. Snorting shit like that
                    at your age, you oughta ---

                              GINA
                    What are you -- a priest? A
                    cop! Look at your life. You
                    can't tell me what to do!

                              TONY
                    I'm telling ya! I don't wanna
                    see you in here again. I catch
                    you in here I'm gonna beat the
                    shit outta you.

                              GINA
                    Oh yeah! Go ahead!

                              TONY
                    You're getting outta here
                    right now! Don't push me baby,
                    don't push me!

                              GINA
                    Don't fucking push me!

                              MANNY
                    Okay, c'mon, let's go outside
                    get some air...

The argument has moved across the bathroom to
the lip of the hallway. Several more people
are watching.

                    GINA
          You got a nerve, Tony, you got
          a nerve! You can't tell me
          what to do. I'll do what I
          want to do. I'll go out with
          who I want and if I want to
          fuck them then I'll fuck them!

Tony, raging, smacks her the face. She reels
back across into the toilet.

Tony stands there, abated.

The crowd is silent.

Manny moves across the floor and kneels down,
consoles Gina who is sobbing.

                    MANNY
          (tender)
          Come on, baby, it's okay, it's
          okay, he didn't mean it.
          (strokes her face)

                    TONY
          (disturbed, to Manny)
          Get her home, get her outta
          here!

He turns and bulldozes his way through the
growing crowd, no regrets, but disturbed.

Manny helps Gina to her feet.

                    MANNY
          Come on, pussycat, I'll buy
          you a cup of coffee.

          CUT TO


110   INT. BABYLON CLUB - MAIN ROOM - NIGHT

Tony, isolated and edgy, reenters the main
room, circling the edges of the crowd, up to
the bar.

                    TONY
          (to the bartenderess, pointing)
          Gimme a double of that!

He turns, catches a last glimpse of Gina
leaving with Manny.

111     EXT. MIAMI STREETS - NIGHT

        Manny drives Gina home in his two-seater
        Mercedes sports coupe. She's still angry.

                    GINA
          ...He's got a nerve the way he
          acts! Mama's right. She says
          he hurts everything he
          touches. Well he's not gonna
          hurt me anymore. He'll never
          see me again. Never!

                    MANNY
          He loves you, what do you
          want. He feels he raised you.

                    GINA
          He still thinks I'm fifteen.
          He's been in jail five years
          and he still thinks I'm
          fifteen!

                    MANNY
          Hey, you're the best thing
          he's got. The only thing. He
          don't want you to grow up to
          be like him. So he's got this
          father thing for you, protect
          you...

                              GINA
                    Against what?


                              MANNY
                    'Gainst assholes -- like the
                    sleaze ball in the red suit.

          He says it like it's personal.

                              GINA
                    (picks up on it)
                    I like Fernando, he's a nice
                    guy, he knows how to treat a
                    woman.


                              MANNY
                    (a face)
                    What future's he got? On a
                    bandstand somewhere? He's a
                    bum, why don't you go out
                    with somebody who's going
                    somewhere?

          She gives him a look.

                              GINA
                    Like who?


                              MANNY
                    Like a doctor or a dentist or
                    something.


                              GINA
                    What about you? Why don't you
                    take me out?

          She's looking straight at him now,
          challenging.

                              MANNY
                    What? Me?

                         GINA
              Yeah, you. I see the way you
              look at me -- Manolo Ribera.

                         MANNY
              (nervous)
              Hey, Tony's like my brother.
              You're his kid sister, okay?

                         GINA
              So what?

                         MANNY
              So...

                         GINA
              (taunting)
              You afraid of Tony? You afraid
              of Tony's kid sister?

                         MANNY
              Fuck no...

112    EXT. TONY'S MOTHER'S HOUSE - NIGHT

              Pulls the car over to the curb.

                         MANNY
              I guess we're here.

       Pause.

                         GINA
              You think about it, okay, you
              think about it real hard,
              Manny. 'Cause you don't know
              what you're missing...

       She leans across the front seat and lightly
       lays a challenging kiss on his cheek. The
       ladykiller is rigid in his terror.

She gets out of the car, crosses in front of his headlights, towards the house, looking at him.

He watches.

CUT BACK TO

113    INT. BABYLON CLUB - LATER THAT NIGHT

The Owner appears at the mike, the music drifting to Sinatra's "Strangers In The Night".

                    OWNER
          All right, you coneheads,
          another exciting evening at
          the Babylon, hunh? Now I want
          you to check out this next
          hombre. I found him stoned in
          the jungle and there's nothing
          you'll ever see like him. I
          present with great pride, from
          Caracas, Venezuela 'Octavia'!

Lights dimming to the bluesy rhythm of the Sinatra song as sad-eyed Octavia suddenly appears in the shifting spotlight drawing immediate laughter.

He is dressed as an enormously fat old man with a Quasimodo mask covering both the front and back of his head and neck.

With a red bulb for a nose, he gyrates grotesquely to the sleek song; once the mood of laughter has been established, the music suddenly shifts upbeat to "Saturday Night Fever" and the clown, like a butterfly from a worm, starts shedding the stuffing from his clothes, his big eyes staring out at us in theatrical melancholy. Tony watches, sitting alone, distracted by the clown. More laughter, more clothes coming off, building a tempo. When the head mask comes off, we see the gaunt handsome face of a young clown in white paint with the large blackened eyes staring without expression at the laughing audience.

Tony is hooked by the image, looks on. The clown is down to his leotards, thin as a stick, and pulling the girls out onto the floor to dance with him, bouncing around like yo-yos. Everybody is laughing, everybody is merry except Tony and the clown, weaving in and out of the sharpening spotlight in his white face as the act comes to its close, a haunting figure of mockery...

Tony, absorbed by his thoughts, is lucky this time. His antennae warn him. Out of the side of his eye, he sees...

The two hitters moving on him.

He sprawls. Machine gun fire rips through the upholstery, smashing the mirrors...

Screams, crowd diving for cover...

Tony, hit in the shoulder, rolls, gets his Baretta out of his ankle, firing...

Hits one of the gunmen in the chest; the man staggers across the disco floor firing volleys into the mirrors and ceilings...

Tony moving under the tables, towards the door, firing...

The second hitter is pinned, firing back, breaking more mirrors, and more screaming.

Tony lets the gunman have another burst then runs out the door, his clothes ripped with blood and glass.

The clown, Octavia, lies dead on the silent dance floor.

114     EXT. THE BABYLON CLUB - NIGHT

Tony runs out, crouched, to his red Jaguar. Exchanging shots with a third hitter across the parking lot, he runs out of ammunition.

He jumps into the Jaguar, his windows being blown out. The second hitter, wounded, running out of the club, towards him.

The third hitter advancing, carhops scattering. Tony reaching under his seat, gets a hold of his own Ingram machine pistol, cocks it and lays down a field of fire. Carhops scattering, the hitters seeking cover.

Hitter two, already wounded, is hit again, his head exploding like squashed watermelon.

Tony now pops a button. Bulletproof blackout shutters whap across the shattered windows. He guns the Jaguar out into the lot, bullets careening off the armor plating, whining against the shutters.

Tony suddenly brakes the car and reaches down and slams the gear shift into reverse.

In an instant, his warmobile accelerates in reverse, climbing to top speed...

As hitter three realizes it's too late, tries to get out of there, but is overtaken and crushed by the car.

CUT TO

115     INT. SAFE HOUSE - THAT NIGHT

        Tony, aching from his wound, is attended by a
        Doctor, who reveals to us an ugly wound on his
        rib cage. Tony looks at it, doesn't express a
        reaction.

                        DOCTOR
                It's going to be sore for a
                few months.

                        TONY
        Somebody else gonna be a lot sorer...
        (to Chi-Chi)
        Find out where Lopez is...

CUT TO

116     INT. MIRIAM'S APARTMENT - NIGHT

        Miriam's a tough-looking little chick in
        panties and a tank top with "Cocaine" written
        on it.

                        TONY'S VOICE
                Miriam? Yeah... Tony. Manny
                there?

                        MIRIAM
                Yeah... It's Tony.

        Manny, in bed, is snorting a line of coke off
        a mirror, takes the phone, in good spirits.

                        MANNY
                Tony cono, whatcha doing --
                checking up on me, too?

117     INT. SAFE HOUSE - NIGHT

                              TONY
                    Look, get your fuckin' clothes
                    on and meet me outside Lopez's
                    office in forty-five minutes.
                    That phone booth on 9th. Yeah.
                    Move your ass!

118     INT. MIRIAM'S APARTMENT - NIGHT

                              MANNY
                    What happened!

119     INT. SAFE HOUSE - NIGHT

                              TONY (v.o.)
                    Nothing we can't fix.

        Tony hangs up.

120     INT. MIRIAM'S APARTMENT - NIGHT

                              MANNY
                    (grabs his pants)
                    I gotta go.

                              MIRIAM
                    This is worse than fucking a
                    grasshopper, man.

                              MANNY
                    Hey, I'm better looking.
                    (hits the coke again)
                    Don't do it all, I'll be back
                    later.

        CUT TO

121     INT. SAFE HOUSE - NIGHT

Tony ignores the doctor taping him, checking his watch.

                    TONY
          (to Nick)
          Nick, when we get there, call
          Lopez at three exactly. You
          got that?

                    NICK
          Yeah, don't worry Tony. I got it.

                    TONY
          All you say is you're one of
          the guys at the club --
          'Hello, Mr. Lopez, there was a
          fuckup, he got away...'

                    NICK
          Yeah, Tony, I got it, no
          problem...

    CUT TO

122   INT. LOPEZ MOTORS - NIGHT

          Waldo remains outside, covering the street as
          Tony, Manny and Chi-chi move gingerly along
          the darkened showroom... Lopez's voice on the
          phone through the half-opened office door.

                    LOPEZ'S VOICE
          ...you're kidding! Three to
          two? Son of a bitch!...
          (cradling the phone)
          Guess what. My softball team,
          y'know, the Little Lopezers?
          They won the Division tonight.
          We're going to Sarasota for
          the State Championship...
          Hunh!

                    MUFFLED VOICE
          Congratulations. That's great
          Frank.


     Tony, Manny and Chi-chi slide into the room,
     the latter two with guns casually drawn.


123    INT. LOPEZ MOTOR'S OFFICE - NIGHT

                    TONY
          Yeah, it sure is Frank. What'd
          you do -- fix the umpire?

     Lopez, his nose in a glass of scotch, almost
     muffs it right there and then, but manages to
     recover.

                    LOPEZ
          Tony...? Uh, I'll call you
          back... yeah.

     Hangs the phone up and rocks forward at his
     desk.

     Lopez's bodyguard, Ernie, gets the message from
     Chi-chi sliding along the wall next to him,
     Manny covering the other side of the room.

                    LOPEZ
          Tony... what happened to you,
          hunh?

                    TONY
          Yeah, lookit. They spoiled one
          of my $800 suits.

                    LOPEZ
          Jesus! Who?

     Tony, in his ripped suit, shoulder in a sling,
     face cut, shifts his eyes with camera slowly

144

onto Mel Bernstein sitting there with a bourbon on the rocks, his two hundred and fifty pounds bulging with irritated surprise.

                    TONY
          Hitters. Somebody musta
          brought 'em in. Never seen 'em
          before... Hiya Mel. Is there
          an answer to this too?

                    BERNSTEIN
          (uneasy)
          Always is Montana, always
          is...

                    LOPEZ
          Jesus, Tony, maybe it was the
          Diaz Brothers, they got a deep
          beef going back to the 'Sun
          Ray' thing.

                    TONY
          Hey, you might be right.

                    LOPEZ
          Anyway I'm glad you made it
          Tony, we'll return the favor
          for you. In spades.

                    TONY
          (sits at the edge of Lopez's
          desk)
          Nah, I'm gonna take care of
          this myself.

Pause.

                    LOPEZ
          (awkward)
          Well... What are the guns for
          Tony?

                    TONY
          (shrugs)
          What for? I'm paranoid I
          guess.

The phone rings.

Lopez lets the phone ring.

                    TONY
          Why don't you answer it Frank?

                    LOPEZ
          Must be Elvira. You know
          women. After we left that
          joint she...

The phone rings again.

                    TONY
          (reaches for it)
          I'll tell her you're not here.

                    LOPEZ
          (grabs the phone first)
          Wait a minute! I'll talk to
          her. Hello?
          (anxious)
          Yeah... all right honey, don't
          worry... I'll be home in an
          hour.

He hangs up. Pause.

                    TONY
          Frank, you're a piece of shit.

                    LOPEZ
          Whatcha talking 'bout Tony?

Tony, angry now, grabs Lopez by the shirt and hauls him forward across his desk so his gut lies flat across it.

                    TONY
          You know what I'm talking
          about you fuckin' cockroach!

                    LOPEZ
          Tony, no! Listen!

                    TONY
          You remember what a 'haza' is
          Frank? It's a pig that don't
          fly straight. Neither do you,
          Frank.

                    LOPEZ
          (nervous)
          Why would I hurt you, Tony,
          I brought you in! So we had a
          few differences, no big deal.
          I gave you your start Tony, I
          believed in you!

                    TONY
          Yeah and I stayed loyal to
          you, Frank. I made what I
          could on the side but I never
          turned you Frank, never -- but
          you -- a man ain't got no
          word, he's a cockroach!

He squashes an imaginary cockroach right in front of Frank's eyes, then pulls him further across the desk, flailing.

                    LOPEZ
          Mel! Mel! Do something, please!

Mel sits there impassively.

MEL

It's your tree Frank, you're
sitting in it.

LOPEZ

Please Tony okay all right!
Gimme a second chance! Ten
million. I'll give you ten
million dollars right now! I
got it in a vault. In Spain.
We'll get on a plane. It's
yours, all of it... Elvira?
You want Elvira? She's yours,
okay! I go away Tony, I
disappear, you'll never see me
again. Just gimme a chance,
gimme a second chance Tony,
please... please!

He sobs pathetically.

LOPEZ

I don't wanna die Tony,
I never did nothing to
nobody Tony! I never hurt
nobody!

TONY

Yeah you're right Frank, you
always had somebody else do it
for you.

He turns to Manny.

TONY

Manny, you mind shooting this
piece of shit for me?

MANNY

Nah.

Tony steps aside.

                    LOPEZ
          No! No! Tony!

Manny shoots him with the silencer. Three
times.

Lopez crashes backwards, draped over his desk
like Marat in his bathtub, amid his patriot
flag and his Kennedy photographs.

                    TONY
          ...Every dog has his day.

He fixes his eyes on Mel Bernstein.

                    BERNSTEIN
          (remaining calmly in his
          chair)
          I told him it didn't make
          sense -- clipping you when he
          coulda had you working for us
          instead. But he got hot
          tonight, y'know, about the
          broad. He fucked up.

                    TONY
          Yeah, so did you, Bernstein.

His eyes... Bernstein, reading them,
gets worried.


                    BERNSTEIN
          Now wait a minute, Montana,
          don't go too far.

                    TONY
          I'm not Mel. You are.

He produces his Baretta from his sling and holds it in his left hand pointed at the big man.

                    BERNSTEIN
               (rising from his chair)
               Hey, c'mon, what is this? You
               can't shoot a cop, Tony.

                    TONY
               Whoever said you were one?

He fires.

Bernstein takes it in the gut, hits the floor, looks up astonished.

                    BERNSTEIN
               I... lemme go, Tony, I can fix
               things up...

                    TONY
               Sure you can chico. Maybe
               you can handle one of them
               first-class tickets to the
               Resurrection. So long, Mel,
               have a good trip.

He fires several times into him until we can imagine he is no longer of the living. Tony turns towards the door.

                    MANNY
               (indicatize bodyguard)
               What about him?

Tony notices.

The bodygurad, Ernie, the middle-aged Cuban, waits stoically.

                              TONY
            You want a job Ernie?

                              ERNIE
            Sure, Tony.

                              TONY
            Come see me tomorrow.

                              ERNIE
            Thanks, Tony.

       Tony walks out alone into the darkened
       showroom, past the hulks of the used
       Cadillacs, as we see the shadows of Manny
       and Chi-Chi moving in a stream of light.

                              MANNY (O-S.)
            Okay, torch it!

   CUT TO

124   INT. LOPEZ CONDO - THAT NIGHT

       Elvira lies in her silk sheets. The doorbell
       rings. She gets up.

       In a nightgown, she opens the front door.

                              ELVIRA
            Tony?...

       Tony, still in his ruined suit with the arm in
       a sling, moves past her into the apartment.

                              ELVIRA
            What's happened?

       Tony just stands there.

                    ELVIRA
          Where's Frank?

                    TONY
          Where do you think? Why don't
          you go pack your stuff. We're
          going home.

     Pause. She understands, moves quietly past him
     towards the bedroom.

     Tony ambles over to the windows and steps out
     on the terrace, breathing in the air. The
     lights of Miami wink at his feet... the camera
     moving to one sign down there that says it
     all, flashing its big neon bracelet ---

                **THE WORLD IS YOURS.**
     PAN AMERICAN TO EUROPE, AFRICA, SOUTH AMERICA

     Tony drinks it in.

     CUT TO

     Montage - Passing Time:

125  MULTI - SCREEN IMAGES

     Spin to lively, marching music.

126  HANDS

     counting money.

127  HANDS

     sealing cocaine bags... quaaludes...
     marijuana.

128  EXT. SOSA VILLA - DAY

Sosa on the phone in Bolivia.

129     INT. TONY'S MANSION - DAY

Tony on the phone in Miami.

130     EXT. MONTANA REALTY - DAY

Tony -- with Manny, Gaspar, and Ernie --
exits the Montana Realty Company in Little
Havana.

131     EXT. MONTANA DIAMOND TRADING COMPANY - DAY

Tony -- with Manny, Gaspar and Gigi -- enters
the Montana Diamond Trading Company in Little
Havana.

132     EXT. GASPAR'S STREET - DAY

One of the Marielitos, is ambushed and blown
up in his car.

133     EXT. BANK - DAY

Camera moving from a sign saying "Banco Del
Sur Miami" to Chi-Chi and Rafi unloading
duffel bags from the back of a Volkswagen van
in the parking lot of the bank. Tony and Manny
supervise... the four of them now moving
towards the bank bent under their weights-like
a column of ants carrying the sugar.

Tony shaking hands in an office with a young
bank president (to be seen again). They sit
down to talk.

135     INT. MANNY'S APARTMENT - DAY

Manny's on the other end -- with another
ladyfriend, both stripped down, the camera

                    moving back down the telephone cord to the
                    receiver...

          CUT TO

136    INT. TAP TRAILER - DAY

                    The tap -- trailer -- simultaneous... the
                    camera moving along the tape spools to the
                    two narc s listening.

137    EXT. STASH HOUSE - NIGHT

                    Rafi, another Marielito, is led off in
                    handcuffs from a suburban stash house by
                    the cops.

138    NEWSPAPER HEADLINES

                    *Time Magazine covers.*
                    "Raid Nets $100 Million Cocaine Stash!"

139    VIC, THE NEWSCASTER ON TV

                    "135 drug-related homicides so far this year!"

139-A  NICK THE PIG

                    shaking down punk in Cuban park.

139-B  LITTLE HAVANA - NIGHT - GINA

                    exits flashy car.

140    OMITTED

141    HANDS

                    stripping false bottoms from suitcases.

142    EXT. GINA'S BEAUTY SALON - DAY

Gina, with Tony, Manny, Waldo, Hernando, Gigi and Elvira looking on, cuts the ribbon for the new Gina Beauty Salons in Little Havana. She looks towards her brother, then her eyes linger on Manny. He suppresses his smile, winks at her.

143     INT. MENS' CLOTHINGSTORE - DAY

Manny buying new suit...

144     INT. TONY'S MOTHER'S KITCHEN - DAY

Mama washing dishes, looking up at the clock.

145     INT. TONY'S BEDROOM - NIGHT

Elvira snorting.

146     OMITTED

147     INT. AMUSEMENT ARCADE - DAY

And Hernando, another of the Marielitos, now sprawls dead over a video machine in an amusement arcade.

148     EXT. MIAMI BEACH

...and a bloated Cigi floats in from the ocean onto the lush white surf of Miami Beach, alongside some kids playing with their shovels.

149     INT. MORGUE - DAY

...as the morgue piles up with rows of corpses, their tagged toes sticking out from under the white sheets like used cars.

...and the beat goes on.

CUT TO

150    EXT. TONY'S MANSION — MORNING - DAY

In an exclusive area of Coral Gables,
surrounded by walls, security gates, acres
of lawns and a guarded boat dock on a canal.
Tony has erected his fortress-like Shangri-La,
to which he has -- with a sense of humor --
added a large neon sign on the front lawn
that says:

        THE WORLD IS YOURS

        MONTANA TRAVEL CO.

Just like it should be.

...as Tony and Elvira take their marriage
vows in front of the Monsignor; the triumphant
montage music rising to its full glory as a
beggar's banquet of gang members and various
girl friends (but no sign of kids) looks on.
Chi-Chi is with a girl who looks like an
animal, with an extremely short dress,
looping earrings, the camera moving to Gina,
her eyes covertly tracking to Manny who gazes
back at her, evenly and openly as...

Tony and Elvira kiss.

151    EXT. TONY'S GROUNDS — SAME DAY

Tony, eating his wedding cake, his arm around
Elvira, nuzzling her, shows his entourage his
new hobby.

Across a moat of water, a striped nine-foot
Bengal tiger stretches majestically under a

solitary banyan tree, extending a giant claw
and licking himself.

Tony and Chi-Chi kidding around with the
tiger.

Intercut to:

151-A EXT. TONY'S MANSION - GUARD HOUSE - DAY

Behind some nearby bushes, Gina and Manny are
making out in the grass. They hear the sounds
of Tony's voice, freeze, making shushing
signals, then almost laugh when they consider
their childish state.

From their point of view, we see Tony leading
the entourage back to the mansion as Chi-Chi
throws the Bengal his wedding cake.

CUT TO

151-B INT. TONY'S MANSION OFFICE - DAY - MONTH LATER

Tony, accompanied by Manny, walks a young,
thirtyish bank president into his office,
which is rigged with video monitors
surveilling all areas of the house and
grounds. There's an abundance of electronics
-- televisions, sound systems, computer toys,
video games, desk, couch, chairs -- but not
one sign of a book on the walls.

Jerry, the Banker, is slickly dressed, hair
coiffed, the eyes scooting shrewdly back and
forth, the type of guy who follows the Hong
Kong money markets on weekends, a guy who
never stops thinking money.

                    TONY
          ...yeah, well, I can't pay

that no more Jerry, I'm gonna
be bringing in more'n I ever
brung in, y'know. I'm talking
ten million a month now.
That's serious money. So I
think it's time you bank boys
come down a bit, y'know,
like...

                    BANKER
Hey, Tony, c'mon, that's
crazy, can't do...

                    TONY
That's too bad, 'cause...

                    BANKER
Tony, sweetheart, we're
not a wholesale operation
here, we're a legitimate
bank. The more cash you give
us the harder it is to rinse,
y'know. The fact is we can't
even take anymore of your
money 'less we raise the
rates on you.

                    TONY
You gonna **what**, Jerry?

                    BANKER
Tony, Tony, we gotta. The IRS
is coming down heavy on South
Florida, y'know. That *Time
Magazine* cover didn't help
any. We gotta do it. Tony, we
got stockholders, we gotta go
ten percent on the first
twelve million; that's in
denominations of twenty. We'll
go eight percent on your ten

dollar bills and six points on
your fives.

                    TONY
Ten points!

                    MANNY
Hey, Tony, we go someplace
else.

                    BANKER
Tony, Tony -- it's no
conspiracy, we're all doing
it. You're not gonna find a
better deal.

                    TONY
Then fuck you, I'll fly the
cash to the Bahamas myself.

                    BANKER
You gonna fly it yourself,
Tony -- on a regular basis?
Once maybe. And then what? You
gonna trust some monkey in a
Bahamian bank with twenty
million of your hard-earned
dollars? C'mon Tony, don't be
a schmuck -- who else can you
trust? That's why you pay us
what you do -- you **trust** us.

Tony looks broodingly. Jerry glances at his
watch, suggesting he has another engagement.

                    BANKER
Stay with us, you're an old
and well-liked customer.
You're in good hands with us
gentlemen, I gotta run. How's
married life? Say hello to the

princess for me -- okay. She's
beautiful. See you. Take care.

Going. Tony watches, raging inside. He pulls a
drawer open and reaches for a private cocaine
supply. It's the first indication we have of
this. As he snorts:

                    TONY
          That prick, that WASP whore.
          What's he think I am, some
          maricon come over on a boat...

                    MANNY
          So why don't we talk to this
          Jew Seidelbaum?  He's got his
          own exchange, he charges four
          percent tops — and he's
          connected.

                    TONY
          I don't know. Mob guys —
          guineas -- I don't trust 'em.

On the video monitor, Tony watches Jerry, the
Banker, leaving. Now beginning to see things
through the glass darkly, Tony hits the other
nostril quickly, casually -- passing the vial
to Manny who does his hit.

                    TONY
          (eyes wandering across to
          another video monitor)
          You get the house sweeped
          this month? The cars?

                    MANNY
          Yeah, sure, I told you that.
          Five thousand it set us back.

TONY

See that cable truck there?


152   INT. TONY'S MANSION OFFICE - DAY - VIDEO MONITORS


Tony's eyes fixing on the cable TV truck
parked across the street. A man is hauling
cable. There are other private gates visible.
The area is lush with gardens, Spanish moss,
cypresses and quietly respectable million
dollar houses with their Spanish tile roofs
and balconies.

MANNY

Yeah?

TONY

Hey Manny when does it take
three days to rig a cable,
hunh?

MANNY

Cops.

TONY

What if it's the Diaz
brothers? What if they're
gonna come and get me?

MANNY

I'll check it out.

TONY

You check it out, then we're
gonna blow that fuckin' truck
back to Bogota.

MANNY

The truck could be anything.
We're not the only dopers
living on the block y'know.

                    TONY
          Hey you got some attitude
          y'know Manny -- for a guy in
          charge of my security.

                    MANNY
          Hey I'll check it out. I'm
          just telling you we're
          spending too much on this
          counter-surveillance shit.
          Twelve percent y'know, of
          our adjusted gross -- that's
          not pocket money.

                    TONY
          You worry about it, it lets me
          sleep good at night. There's
          that fat guy again.

Manny looks over at a jogger running by the
gate -- of the porcine quality, civilian-
looking, fifties.

                    TONY
          I seen him every day. 'Bout a
          week now.

                    MANNY
          So the guy jogs around the
          neighborhood. He's some fat
          accountant.

                    TONY
          How the fuck do you know what
          he is?

                    MANNY
          Hey if he's a cop don't you
          think running in circles
          around a house is a pretty
          dumb way to watch it?

                              TONY
                    Maybe not...
                    (walks away, stops, looks
                    back)
                    I'm telling you we're getting
                    sloppy -- our thinking -- our
                    attitude. We're not fucking
                    hungry anymore!

A-158 EXT. TONY'S MANSION - NIGHT - ESTABLISHING SHOT

158   INT. TONY'S MANSION - BATHROOM - NIGHT - CLOSE ON
      TELEVISION COMMERCIAL

                    A television spot for Florida Security Trust
                    (or Miami Security Trust or Dade Security Trust
                    depending on legal options). A respectable
                    business-type walks along the sidewalk with
                    a renascent downtown Miami as a backdrop.
                    Skyscrapers, glinting glass, cranes...

                              BANK SPOKESMAN
                    Here at Florida Security Trust
                    we've been putting your money
                    to work for a better America.
                    We've been around for seventy-
                    five years. We'll be here
                    tomorrow.

                    A logo for the firm over with the reminder
                    "Since 1907."

                    Camera pulling back to reveal Tony watching in
                    his huge goldleaf bathtub, a cigar clenched
                    between his teeth. He looks like a character
                    in a *Futzie Nutzie* loafing cartoon, with his
                    TV hooked to one side of the tub, a long phone
                    line to the other, and a radio and portable
                    bar all within reach.

                    TONY
          (to the TV)
          Yeah that's 'cause for
          seventy-five years you been
          fucking all of us over,
          that's why.
          (to Manny)
          Somebody oughta do something
          about these whores. Charging
          me ten points on my money
          and they're getting away with
          it! There's no laws anymore,
          anything goes.


                    MANNY
          Listen, these guys been here
          for a thousand years. They got
          all the angles figured.


Manny straddles a chair next to the tub
watching the TV news that was interrupted by
the Florida Security Trust commerical. Behind
him Elvira's in a robe, fixing herself up in
front of a giant mirror. It's some bathroom --
gigantic with a chandelier hanging in the
middle of it, rugs, Italian marble, plants,
skylights, etc...


                    TONY
          You know what capitalism is --
          Getting fucked.


                    ELVIRA
          A true capitalist if ever I
          met one.


She's doing a toot of coke off a flat mirror.


                    TONY
          How would you know, bubble-
          head? You ever do nothing

    'sides get your hair fixed and
    powder your nose? You do too
    much of that shit anyway.

           ELVIRA
    Nothing exceeds like excess.
    You should know that Tony.

           TONY
    Know what? Why do you always
    got to talk like that?

           MANNY
    (changing the subject)
    So I had a pow-wow with this
    guy Seidelbaum today. He
    checks out. I got another meet
    set up.

           TONY
    When?

           MANNY
    Thursday ten o'clock. I
    thought I'd take Chi-Chi with
    me. Do a million and some
    change. Get my feet wet with
    this guy.

           TONY
    That's a lot of wet. I'm not
    Rockefeller. Not yet.

Tony points to a figure on the TV.

           TONY
    Hey, listen to this, guy's
    always good for a laugh.

Visual of silver-haired television Anchorman
-- Vic Phillips -- with a bit of show business

image in him -- to be seen again. Underneath
his face, it says "Editorial."

                    NEWS ANCHORMAN
          ...the question is how with a
          small law enforcement budget
          do you put a **dent** in an
          estimated $100 billion a year
          business? It seems at times
          all you can do is put your
          finger in the dike and pray
          but now we are hearing voices
          that say the only way we can
          solve the drug problem is the
          same way Prohibition was
          solved. Not by outlawing the
          substances but by legalizing
          and taxing them. These voices
          say that will drive out the
          organized crime element...
          (pause for effect)
          I am **not** one of those voices.

                    TONY
          (responding)
          What do you know -- you never
          been right in your life, Vic
          baby...
          (to Manny)
          Guy never fuckin' tells
          the truth. It's the guys like
          him, the bankers and the
          politicians who want to keep
          the coke illegal so's they can
          make more money and get the
          votes to fight the bad guys.
          They're the bad guys. **They'll**
          fuck anything for a buck...

                    ELVIRA
          And what about you Tony?

Can't you stop talking about
it all the time, can't you
stop saying fuck? -- it's
boring, it's **boring**!

                TONY
What's boring?

                ELVIRA
You're boring. Money, money,
money! That's all I hear in
this house. Frank never talked
about money.

                TONY
'Cause Frank was dumb.

                ELVIRA
You know what you've become
Tony -- an arriviste, an
immigrant spic millionaire who
can't stop talking... about
how much money he's got or how
he's getting fucked. Why don't
you just dig a hole in the
garden honey and bury it and
forget it.

                TONY
What're you talking about, I
worked my ass off for all
this.
(indicates the bathroom)

                ELVIRA
(starts out)
It's too bad. Somebody
should've given it to you. You
would've been a nicer person.

                    TONY
          Hey you know what your problem
          is pussycat...

                    ELVIRA
          (at the lip of the bathroom)
          What is my problem, Tony?

                    TONY
          ...you got nothing to do with
          your life that's what.

                    MANNY
          Tony, c'mon...

                    TONY
          Why don't you get a job
          y'know? Be a nurse, work
          with blind kids, lepers,
          open a stationary store, I
          don't give a shit. Anything
          beats lying around waiting
          for me to fuck you all the
          time.

                    ELVIRA
          (stung)
          Don't toot your horn, you're
          not that good.

                    TONY
          Frank was better?

                    ELVIRA
          (quietly)
          You're an asshole.

     She goes.

                              TONY
              (calling after her, guilty)
              Hey c'mon Elvie, whatta we
              fight for, this is dumb!

He splashes the water in his tub and slams the
TV shut.

                             MANNY
              (watching)
              I guess married life's not all
              that it's cracked up to be,
              hunh, chico?

A friendly smile but Tony just stares glumly
after Elvira.

                             MANNY
              (rises)
              I gotta hot date...

                              TONY
              (glaring into his bathwater)
              This Seidelbaum thing?

                             MANNY
              Yeah?

                              TONY
              Me and Nick'll take care of
              it. You stay out of it.

                             MANNY
              (very surprised)
              It's my deal. Why!

                              TONY
              You stink as a negotiator,
              that's why. You like the
              ladies more'n you do the money
              -- that's your problem Manny.

                    MANNY
          Hey wait a second, I'm your
          partner Tony, you can't trust
          me, who the fuck can you
          trust?

     Pause. Tony mumbles something, barely heard.

                    TONY
          **Junior** partner.

                    MANNY
          (catching)
          Junior partner my ass!

                    TONY
          I'm in charge. Do as I say.
          You go to Atlanta, you handle
          the Gomez delivery there.

                    MANNY
          (a beat)
          You oughta listen to your wife,
          muchacho. You **are** an asshole.

     He leaves, pissed, Tony mumbling to himself in
     his bath.

                    TONY
          (to himself)
          Fuck you too... what do you
          know, who the hell put things
          together... me! Who do I trust
          -- me, that's who...

DISSOLVE TO


159  EXT. WAREHOUSE - ALONGSIDE MIAMI FREEWAY - DAY

          Tony and Nick The Pig get out of a van,
          frowning in the glary sunlight. From the

continual sound of jet aircraft taking off and
landing we might sense we're near an airport.
As Nick hauls a duffel bag on his back, Tony,
carrying a suitcase of his own, reads the sign
on top of the warehouse:

"CONSOLIDATED CARRIES INC."

160    INT. SEIDELBAUM OFFICE - WAREHOUSE - DAY

The office is bare and ugly, the furniture
naugahyde black. There's noise from an outer
office, and people on phones, moving, talking.

Tony and Nick sit on a couch stacking twenty
dollar bills from the duffel bag and suitcase
onto a coffee table.

Two men in casual sports clothing sit opposite
them in chairs, one of them -- Seidelbaum --
squaring the bills and passing them
efficiently through a money-counting machine
which clicks at rhythmic intervals throughout
the scene. Seidelbaum's a small, fat 7th
Avenue-type with a lot of rings on his
fingers and sharp, porky eyes.

The other guy -- Luis -- a dark Cuban, is
long, lean and smooth with aquiline nose and
dancing eyes. He drinks coffee, smiles a lot
and bullshits -- two sordid guys who look the
part. It's a tedious process counting a
million five in twenties, it takes four/five
hours; and throughout the desultory dialogue
Tony, absorbed by the money, and Nick never
stop the monotonous work of counting and
stacking and noting the amounts. At all times
all four men, thoroughly aware of the large
stacks on the table, move and talk gingerly
although they appear casual and bored. They
drink a lot of coffee.

                         LUIS
              ...yeah back then I worked in
              pictures down in Columbia. I
              was in that picture *Burn*,
              y'ever see it?... with Marlon
              Brando. We're good friend. I
              was his driver...

                         NICK
              (stacking)
              Oh yeah?

                         LUIS
              Yeah, in Caragena, they shot it
              there... Gillo Pontecorvo, he
              was the director. Italian guy.
              (pause)
              Yeah, I also know Paul Newman.
              I worked with him in Tucson.

                      NICK THE PIG
              That so? Say, you know Benny
              Alvarez there?

                         LUIS
              Uh...

                      SEIDELBAUM
              (interrupting to Tony)
              Now you want a company check
              here for $283,107.65?

                         TONY
              (pause, checking his fingers)
              Uh... I come up with 284.6

                      SEIDELBAUM
              (pauses, looks again at his
              figures)
              No, that's just not possible.

The machine don't make
mistakes.

                    TONY
          Well, we'll count it again.

                    SIEDELBAUM
          Oh Jesus!

                    TONY
          Hey business is business.
          We're talking $1500.

                    SEIDELBAUM
          (exasperated)
          Okay, you keep the change
          okay, I don't give a shit.

                    TONY
          Okay but I'll go through it
          again with you.

Seidelbaum ignores it, counting up another
stack.

                    SEIDELBAUM
          Okay... This check now, this
          one goes to the...

                    TONY
          Montana Realty Company.

                    NICK
          (to Luis)
          How come you don't know Benny
          Alvarez?

DISSOLVE TO


161   INT. SEIDELBAUM'S WAREHOUSE OFFICE - DAY

They're drinking another round of coffee,
exhausted, smoke filling the room. The table
now resembles a Mount Everest of green and
they're still counting. The money, like
discarded food, is spread all over the place
-- in boxes, brown paper bags, on the couch.
They stretch, rub their eyes.

                    SEIDELBAUM
          We're up to what?

                    LUIS
          (consulting his notes)
          Seven checks. A million three
          hundred twenty-five and six
          hundred twenty-three... plus
          eighteen cents.

                    TONY
          (grins)
          Hey we're almost finished.
          Another 200 thousand and we
          can take a leak.

                    SIEDELBAUM
          Yeah but this'll do fine.

Pulls a pistol from his ankle and rises.

                    SEIDELBAUM
          You're under federal arrest,
          Montana, for a continuing
          criminal conspiracy. The Rico
          Statute. Get 'em up.

Tony astonished.

                    TONY
          Oh shit. You're not kidding
          hunh?

Eyes darting. Considering the options. The
little fat man's eyes are suddenly agile and
mean -- Tony reads them, lifts his arms.

                    SEIDELBAUM
          (to Luis)
          Get it.

Luis moves around Tony to disarm him.

                    TONY
          So how do I know you guys are
          cops?

Luis, produces a wallet with identification,
shoves it under Tony's nose.

                    LUIS
          What's that say, asshole?

Insert: Photograph and Drug Enforcement Agency ID.

                    TONY
          (impressed)
          Hey that's good work, where
          can I get one of those?

                    LUIS
          Cabron! You call yourself
          Cuban? You make a real Cuban
          throw up.

                    SEIDELBAUM
          Looie! Cool it.

                    TONY
          (unfazed; wiping the sweat
          off)
          Call your dog off, Seidelbaum.
          I wanna call my lawyer.

                              SEIDELBAUM
                    Lotta good he's gonna do you
                    Montana. There's an eye there
                    in the wall.
                    (points)
                    Say hi, honey...

162    INT. SEIDELBAUM'S WAREHOUSE OFFICE - DAY -
       REVERSE ANGLE ON VIDEOTAPE

            Blurry image of the men in the room. Tony is
            not that clear an image as he glances briefly,
            uninterested, into the camera.

                              TONY
                    Yeah, is that what you jerk
                    off in front of Seidelbaum?

                              NICK
                    Oh shit and I was supposed to
                    meet this chick at three.
                    What a pain in the ass.

                              SEIDELBAUM
                    (to camera)
                    Okay, Danny, turn it off.

            The angle goes black.

163    BACK TO SCENE

                              SEIDELBAUM
                    (reciting the Miranda)
                    All right, Montana, you have
                    the right to remain silent.
                    Anything you say can be taken
                    against you. You have the...

                              TONY
                    (cuts him off)
                    I know all that shit,

                    Seidelbaum, save your breath.
                    It ain't gonna stick. You
                    know it, I know it. I'm here
                    changing dollar bills is all.
                    So you wanna waste everybody's
                    time here, I call my lawyer.
                    Best lawyer in Miami. He's so
                    good tomorrow morning you're
                    gonna be working in Alaska,
                    Seidelbaum...

          As they handcuff him...

     DISSOLVE TO

164  INT. TONY'S BATHROOM - DAY

                    "Drug King Posts Record $5 Million Bond" --
                    a front page photo of Tony, Elvira, and
                    Sheffield, the lawyer.

     CUT TO

165  INT. TONY'S BATHROOM - DAY

                    Tony, tense, checks himself in the mirror,
                    adjusts his hair. A vial of coke appears.
                    He snorts a large amount, goes out. It's the
                    first time we sense he might be using the
                    stuff on a steady and increasingly heavy
                    basis.

     CUT TO

166  INT. LAWYER'S OFFICE - NIGHT

                    Tony is pacing nervously. Manny looks on.
                    Red-headed Sheffield rasps through a cloud
                    of cigarette smoke behind his desk.

                    SHEFFIELD
          You give me a check for a
          hundred grand plus three hun-
          dred in cash and I guarantee
          you walk on the conspiracy
          charge. But they're gonna come
          back at us on a tax evasion --
          and they'll get it.

                    TONY
          What am I looking at?

                    SHEFFIELD
          Five years, you'll be out in
          three, maybe less if I can
          make a deal.

                    TONY
          For what! Three years in the
          can! For washing money? This
          whole country's built out of
          washed money!

                    MANNY
          Hey, Tony, what's three years?
          It's not like Cuba here. It's
          like going to a hotel.

Tony shakes his head, grimacing like he's
having an epileptic fit.

                    SHEFFIELD
          I'll delay the trial. A year
          and a half, two years, you
          won't start doing time till
          '85.

                    TONY
          No... no, they never get me
          back in a  cage... never!
          Hey, George I go another four

178

hundred grand -- I go 800,000
dollars, okay? With that you
can fix the Supreme Court,
hunh?

                SHEFFIELD
        Tony... the law has to prove
        'beyond a reasonable doubt.'
        I'm an expert at raising that
        doubt but when you got a
        million three undeclared dollars
        staring into a videotape
        camera, honeybaby, it's hard
        to convince a jury you found
        it in a taxi cab.

Tony paces back and forth like a tiger, corking
his fury. Abruptly coming to a decision, he
whirls and leans across Sheffield's desk.

                TONY
        All right -- all right. I do
        the three fuckin' years but
        lemme tell you about my law,
        George. It's real simple.
        There's no 'reasonable doubt.'
        If you're rain-making the
        judge or you fuck me for the
        four hundred grand and I come
        in guilty on the big rap --
        you, the judge, the prosecutor,
        nothing's gonna stop me,
        y'hear? I'm gonna come and tear
        your fuckin' eyeballs out.

Pause.

                SHEFFIELD
        (cool)
        The point is made. Now where's
        the money?

Tony nods to Manny who hauls a briefcase up on
Sheffield's desk. Tony abruptly walks out, a
vial appearing in his hands as he steps out of
the office. He sniffs.

167 EXT. SOSA VILLA - BOLIVIA - DAY

Camera follows Tony with Ernie and Chi-Chi
down the outside gallery onto the veranda
where Sosa is reclining with several other
men -- all in casual clothes, enjoying their
coffee after lunch.

                    SOSA
          (rising)
          Tony... Tony.

                    TONY
          Alex.

They hug like they were the closest of
friends.

                    SOSA
          I'm glad you made it on such
          short notice. I appreciate it.
          How's Elvira?

                    TONY
          She's okay. How's your wife?

                    SOSA
          Three more months.

                    TONY
          That's great.

                    SOSA
          And you, when are you going to
          have another Tony to take your
          place.

                         TONY
               (sore point)
          I'm working on it.


                         SOSA
          I guess you'll have to work
          harder, Tony.


They laugh, nervously. Sosa is a little more
reserved with him than before -- in tune with
the other men at the meeting.


                         SOSA
          Tony, come, I want you to meet
          some friends of mine.


He smoothly guides Tony towards the group of
men who rise.


                         SOSA
          This is Pedro Quinn, chairman
          of Andes Sugar here... Tony
          Montana.


                      PEDRO QUINN
          A pleasure, Mr. Montana.


Camera tracking through ad-lib introductions,
the music assuming a faint martial stride.


                         SOSA
          General Eduardo Strasser,
          Commander of the First Army
          Corps... Tony Montana.


The man is in civilian clothes.


                         SOSA
          Ariel Bleyer, from the
          Ministry of the Interior...
          Tony Montana.

The cameras moving past Sosa's black aide,
the Skull (who nailed Omar) silent behind his
sunglasses, to an American-type in a Brooks
Brothers suit who stands.

                    SOSA
          Charles Goodson -- a friend of
          ours from Washington.

                    TONY
     Hi...

                    GOODSON
          How do you do, Mr. Montana...

He smells like a government guy. Sosa summons
the black aide -- in a hushed voice.

                    SOSA
          Nicky, have Alberto meet us in
          the living room.

The black aide goes.

                    SOSA
          (solicitous)
          Tony, come, please sit here.

Tony is shown a chair in the middle of the
veranda, surrounded on all sides. There is a
strained beat to the proceedings. Ernie and
Chi-Chi hang around the edges.

He suddenly catches a glimpse of the sloe-eyed
Gabriella moving with another woman past a
window of the house. Then she's gone.

Sosa pulls up a chair right opposite Tony,
almost touching knees.

                    SOSA

          Tony, I want to discuss
          something that concerns all
          of us here...

                    TONY

          Sure, Alex.

                    SOSA

          Tony, you have a problem; we
          have a problem... I think we
          can solve both our problems.

Tony waits.

                    SOSA

          We all know you have tax
          troubles in your country --
          and you may have to do a
          little time. But we have some
          friends in Washington who tell
          us these troubles can be taken
          care of... maybe you'll have
          to pay a big fine and some
          back interest, but there's
          no time...

Pause. Tony looks. The American guy, Goodson,
shifts his gaze away.

                    TONY
          And *your* problem, Alex?

Sosa looks around, stands up.

                    SOSA
          Come I I'll show you.

Tony cautiously stands to follow him.

CUT TO

168     INSERT - INT. SOSA VILLA LIVING ROOM - DAY -
        VIDEOTAPE - MATOS STUDY

        A "Phil Donahue-type" setting. A segment now in
        progress with the "Donahue-type" interviewing
        Dr. Orlando Gutierrez. Gutierrez is a young
        charismatic man, very well dressed and
        polished in a South American manner who
        exudes a sense of enormous passion.

                        GUTIERREZ
              More than 10,000 of our people
              are being tortured and held
              without trial. In the past two
              years, another 6,000 have
              simply disappeared. And your
              government -- what does it do?
              It sells my government tanks,
              planes, guns, but not a
              word -- not a whisper -- about
              human rights!

                        INTERVIEWER
              I've heard whispers, Doctor
              Gutierrez, about the financial
              support your government
              receives from the drug
              industry in Bolivia.

                        GUTIERREZ
              The irony, of course, is that
              this money -- which is in the
              billions, Jim -- is coming
              from your country. You are
              the major purchaser of our
              national product -- which of
              course is cocaine.

                    INTERVIEWER
          So what you're saying Doctor
          Gutierrez is the United States
          Government is spending
          millions of dollars to
          eliminate the flow of drugs
          into our streets and at the
          same time is doing business
          with the very same government
          that floods those streets with
          cocaine... that's a bit like
          robbing Peter to pay Paul,
          isn't it?

                    GUTIERREZ
          (laughs)
          Let me show you some of
          the other characters in the
          comedy, Jim... my organization
          just recently traced a
          purchase by this man --

Gutierrez holds up a photograph -- insert the
face on the TV screen, dour, ruthless.

                    GUTIERREZ
          ...here he is, the charming
          face belongs to General
          Cucombre, the Defense Minister
          of my country. Two months ago
          he bought a twelve million
          dollar villa on Lake Lucerne
          in Switzerland. Now if he's
          supposed to be the Bolivian
          Defense Minister, what's he
          doing living in Switzerland?
          Guarding the cash register?

Laughter.

169    TONY

watching, touching his nose a lot, blowing it,
hyped from the coke usage.

                    SOSA
          ...a Communist — financed by
          Moscow.

170    GUTIERREZ

          holds up another photograph — insert the face
          on the TV screen.

                    GUTIERREZ
          ...this is Alejandro Sosa.
          Interesting character. A
          wealthy landowner. Educated in
          England. Good family. The
          business brain and drug
          overlord of an empire stretching
          across the Andes. Not your
          ordinary drug dealer...

                    INTERVIEWER
          What are you suggesting we do
          about this, Doctor?

                    GUTIERREZ
          (passionate)
          The United States Government
          has to stop supporting these
          facist gangsters that are
          running my country, that is
          what your country has to do.
          You have to set a strong
          example by calling for the
          observation of fundamental
          human rights.

171    TONY

staring intently at him, reluctantly
impressed.

                    GUTIERREZ
          You Americans have no idea how
          important your country is as a
          symbol and a bastion of those
          rights. You have no...

Sosa flips off the television. The lights come
on. He's alone with Tony.

                    SOSA
          ...he's scheduled next for *60
          Minutes.* He's going on French,
          British, Italian, Japanese
          television. People everywhere
          are starting to listen to him.
          He's embarrassing, Tony...
          That's our problem.

                    TONY
          Yeah.

Sosa looks up.

The Shadow (seen before at the disposal of
Omar) comes into the room, thin and quiet, his
venomous eyes flicking over Tony. The Skull
leads him in.

                    SOSA
          You've met Alberto before?...

                    TONY
          (remains seated)
          Sure. How could I forget?

                    SOSA
          Alberto, you know Tony Montana
          -- my partner from Florida.

Alberto nods icily, remains standing adjacent.

                    SOSA
          (to Tony)
          So you see Alberto here is
          going to help fix our problem.
          Alberto, you know, is an
          expert in the disposal
          business -- but he doesn't
          know his way around the States
          too well, he doesn't speak
          English, and he needs a little
          help...
          (then)
          Is that a problem, Tony?

Tony looks around the faces, then:

                    TONY
          That's no problem, Alex...

Alex nods, pleased.

Hold on Tony. He blows his nose again.

     CUT TO

172  INT. THE LAUNDRY RESTAURANT - MIAMI - NIGHT

          A millionaire's place, like "The Forge" on
          Arthur Godfrey Road.

          Tony, Elvira, and Manny are shown to their
          table by the maitre'd.

          Tony, a little loaded, intersects a group of
          people at another table and stops, putting his
          hand on a heavyset man's shoulder.

                    TONY
          Hey, Vic, I watch your show
          everyday.

     Vic -- who we saw before editorializing on
     television -- cranes his leonine white head
     of hair around with a patrician annoyance
     reserved for bores in restaurants.

                    VIC
          Oh, is that so?

                    TONY
          Yeah. Hey, you know that two
          hundred kilo DEA bust you was
          congratulating the cops for on
          the tube the other night?

                    VIC
          Aren't you... Tony Montana?

                    TONY
          (beaming now, ignoring Manny
          who comes to retrieve him)
          Yeah, that's me.

     The half-dozen rich people in the dinner party
     are intrigued.

                    TONY
          (waves to them)
          Hi folks, don't get up.
          Anyway, Vic, check it out. I
          heard like it was 220 kilos
          went down. That means twenty
          is missing, right? Ask your
          friends, the cops, about that
          — and keep up the good work,
          Vic, but don't believe
          everything you hear, y'know
          what I mean? Okay, have a

good dinner, nice to meet you
people.

Waves farewell to them, pats Vic once more on
the shoulder, and leaves them murmuring.

> MANNY
> (reproving)
> Hey, Tony, that's not cool,
> he's got a lotta friends in...

> TONY
> I don't give a fuck. He's an
> asshole! Never fucking tells
> the truth on TV! That's the
> trouble in this country. Nobody
> fucking tells the truth!

Not caring if he's overheard, Tony seems
to be in the grip of an anguish he does not
understand.

CUT TO

173     TONY

sits with Manny and Elvira, who is dipping
into a vial of coke in the purse in her lap.
Another huge meal is being consumed, the best
roast beef, bottles of red and white wine,
cigars...

> MANNY
> ...so what's the big mystery,
> what happened down there with
> Sosa?

> TONY
> Lot of bullshit, that's what.
> Politics. The whole world's
> turning into politics.

He pulls out his own vial under the table
between eating and drinking.

                    MANNY
          The one thing we always stayed
          out of was politics, Tony.

                    TONY
          Yeah, so what do you think
          Emilio Rebenga was? Politics
          or what?

Manny remembers.

                    TONY
          No free rides in this world,
          kid.

                    MANNY
          So who's this guy you brought
          back with you, the guy who
          don't blink?

                    ELVIRA
          What guy?

                    TONY
          (to Manny)
          You stay out of it. Run things
          down here. I'll be up in New
          York next week.

He takes a hit, unnoticed.

                    ELVIRA
          (unheard)
          What guy?

                    MANNY
          (to Tony)
          I don't like it.

                    TONY
          You don't like it! It was you
          got me into this mess in the
          first place with that fuckin'
          Seidelbaum!

                    MANNY
          What's Seidelbaum got to do
          with this?

Tony sighs, turning his attention to Elvira.
He surveys the table with the bored satiety of
a Roman Emperor, points to Elvira's untouched
plate.

                    TONY
          Why don't you eat your food,
          what's wrong with it?

                    ELVIRA
          I'm not hungry.

She quickly does one nostril with a quick,
practiced movement of her hand.

                    TONY
          So what'd you order it for?

                    ELVIRA
          I lost my appetite.

She does the other nostril. Tony looking at
her. One beat. Two beats. He passes a silent
burp.

                    MANNY
          (trying to shift the mood)
          So what about the trial? I
          heard Sheffield thinks he can
          get a new postponement...

Tony, bleary-eyed now and drunk, continues to look at Elvira, then away, encompassing the restaurant.

                    TONY
          (ignoring the question)
          Is this it? Is that what it's
          all about, Manny?  Eating,
          drinking, snorting, fucking?
          Then what? You're fifty and
          you got a bag for a belly and
          tits with hair on 'em and your
          liver's got spots and you're
          looking like these rich
          fuckin' mummies in here? Is
          that what it's all about?

                    MANNY
          It's not so bad Tony, could be
          worse...

                    TONY
          (doesn't hear)
          ...is that what I worked for?
          With these hands? Is that what
          I killed for? For this?
          (turns his gaze stonily on
          Elvira)
          A junkie??? I gotta fucking
          junkie for a wife? Who never
          eats nothing, who wakes up
          with a qualude, who sleeps all
          day with black shades on, who
          won't fuck me 'cause she's in
          a coma!

                    MANNY
          (gently)
          Tony, you're drunk.

                    TONY
        ...is this how it ends? And I
        thought I was a winner? Fuck
        it man, I can't even have a
        fucking kid with her, her
        womb's so polluted, I can't
        even have a fucking little
        baby!

Elvira reacts -- wanting to kill. She gets up
and dumps her plate filled with food on him.
Slop drips all over him.

                    ELVIRA
        **You sonufabitch! You fuck!**

They got a black tie audience now. The waiter
tipping around to clean up the mess. Tony
slowly wiping the food off himself.

                    ELVIRA
        How dare you talk to me like
        that! You call yourself a man!
        What makes you so much better
        than me, what do you do? Deal
        drugs? Kill people? Oh that's
        just wonderful Tony — a real
        contribution to human history.
        You want a kid. What kind of
        father do you think you'd
        make, Tony? What kind of
        stories are you going to tell
        the kid before he goes to
        sleep at night? You going to
        drive him to school in the
        mornings, Tony? You really
        think you're still going to be
        alive by the time he goes to
        school, Tony? You're dreaming,
        Tony, you're dreaming!

The audience is hushed, involved, the camera
moving over the faces of Vic and his rich
friends.

Tony acidly quiet, looks around at the people,
back to her.

               TONY
      Sit down before I kill you.

              ELVIRA
      You think of yourself as a
      husband, too, Tony. But did
      you ever stay home without
      having six of your goons
      around all the time? I have
      Nick the Pig as a friend? What
      kind of life is that Tony?
      What kind of life is that?
      (in a softer tone)
      Oh Tony don't you see? Don't
      you see what we've become?
      We're losers, honey, we're not
      winners, we're losers...

Silence. Tony's fury has passed. So has
Elvira's. There's this awkwardness all of a
sudden like two actors who forgot their lines.

               TONY
      (softly)
      Go on, get a cab home, you're
      stoned.
      (to Manny)
      Manny.

              ELVIRA
      No, I'm not stoned Tony.
      You're stoned. You're so
      stoned you don't even know it.

                    TONY
          All right I'm stoned. Manny.


                    MANNY
          (rising, trying to put his arm
          on Elvira)
          Come on, baby.


                    ELVIRA
          No, no you stay right there
          Manny, I'm not going home with
          you... I'm not going home with
          anybody. I'm going home
          alone...
          (staring at Tony)
          I'm leaving you. I don't need
          this shit anymore.


Pause. She starts wobbling out. Past the
silent spectators, their eyes moving between
her and Tony.


Manny rises to follow.


                    TONY
          Let her go!... Another quaalude
          and she'll love me again.


Stumbling once, Elvira disappears out the
door. Tony's eyes follow her. Pause.


The whole room is watching him sitting there
covered with food, the silence cathedral.
He stands, wiping at the food and throwing
several hundred dollar bills on the table,
then looks up angrily at the staring
millionaires.


                    TONY
          You're all assholes. You know
          why? 'Cause none of you got

the guts to be what you want
to be.

He wobbles against the table. Manny tries to
help. Tony shakes him loose.

> TONY
> You need people like me so you
> can point your fingers and say
> 'hey there's the bad guy!' So
> what does that make you? Good
> guys? Don't kid yourselves.
> You're no better'n me. You
> just know how to hide -- and
> how to lie. Me I don't have
> that problem. I always tell
> the truth -- even when I lie.
> He starts out, staggers.

> TONY
> So say good night to the bad
> guy... You're never gonna see
> a bad guy like me again.

He walks out, proud, Manny bringing up the
rear. The room is empty for a beat -- an
extended beat, the stage without its star --
and then the audience begins to buzz with
horror and delight.

CUT TO

174     EXT. GUITERREZ'S STREET - NEW YORK - NIGHT

A quiet East Eighties street. Two rich-looking
male lovers stroll past with their dog. A
moment of silence. Tony moves into frame.

Behind him, the Shadow (Alberto) moves towards
a sedan parked along the curb, carrying an
airline bag. He slips under the car.

Tony looks:

175    ERNIE

       down the street at the intersection of the
       avenue, surveying traffic, signals okay.

176    CHI-CHI

       waits in Tony's sedan double-parked down the
       block.

       Tony, feeling everything's okay, does a
       nervous, quick snort, paces next to the
       vehicle the Shadow disappeared under.

       Ground level -- the Shadow, using a pen
       flashlight, removes the bomb from the bag.
       With subtly inexorable music, the camera
       frames and moves on the bomb -- wired,
       soldered, taped -- a malignant centipede in
       the long agile fingers of the Shadow, who
       delicately presses a tester. A glass button
       on the bomb now flashes red at soothing
       intervals as the Shadow winds a roll of black
       tape from the bomb to an axle of the car.

177    ERNIE

       signals.

178    TONY

       sees it.

       A cop car comes cruising off the avenue up the
       street, towards us.

       Ground level -- the Shadow continues to wind
       his black tape trying to secure the bomb as
       tight as possible.

Tony hurries to the car, bends down.

                    TONY
            (Spanish)
        Psst! La Jara! Apaga.

The Shadow douses it and freezes in position.

Tony looks up just as the cop car pulls
alongside, the passenger cop, a female,
noticing him, saying something to her
partner who eases the car to a halt.

Tony hurries out into the street, taking the
initiative.

                    TONY
        Hey officer, uh you haven't
        seen a little dog have you, a
        little white poodle, it's
        around here somewhere? Jesus
        my kid's gonna go crazy when
        he hears I lost 'im. Oh boy am
        I gonna be in trouble.

                    FEMALE COP
        Why don't you check the ASPCA
        okay? They handle that
        stuff...

                    TONY
        The ASPCA? What's that?..
        Jesus, that's not the place
        where they chop these dogs up
        is it?

                    FEMALE COP
            (in a hurry)
        Look it up in the Yellow Pages
        okay, buddy.

                    (signal to her partner, they
                    drive off)

          Tony looks at them go, takes another snort,
          walks over to the car, bangs on the hood
          several times.

                              TONY
                    Hey smiley, come on outta
                    there, you're under arrest!

          Pause. The Shadow, unsmiling, appears from
          under the car, gun drawn, glowing with
          perspiration. When he realizes it's a joke,
          his eyes blaze at Tony.

                              SHADOW
                    (Spanish)
                    What the fuck you doing!

                              TONY
                    (winks)
                    Hey that was close, hunh?

     CUT TO

179     EXT. GUITERREZ's STREET - NEW YORK - DAY -
        EARLY NEXT MORNING

          Ernie, Chi-Chi, and the Shadow huddle cold and
          uncomfortable in the sedan, waiting -- eating
          pizzas and drinking beers. The morning has
          come down ice cold.

180     INT. PHONE BOOTH - NEW YORK - DAY

          At the phone booth up the corner, Tony —
          unshaven, bleary-eyed - is rapping on the phone.

                              TONY
                    Yeah, yeah... nah, nah... you

tell Sheffield keep his nose
out of it, there's not gonna
be no trial, I got everything
under control, yeah... Have
you heard from Elvira?

He waits, hangs up, snorts some more,
impatient. He picks up the phone again,
starts dialing.

181     INT. TONY'S SEDAN - NEW YORK - DAY

In the sedan, the Shadow peers over, angry, at
Tony.

                    SHADOW
            (Spanish)
            What the fuck's he doing now!
            That sonufabitch...

182     INT. PHONE BOOTH - NEW YORK - DAY

In the booth, Tony, snorting another nostril,
moves back and forth as the phone rings at the
other end. Finally she picks up,

                    ELVIRA'S VOICE
            Yes?

                    TONY
            Hello baby, how's
            Baltimore?... hey look
            Elvira, I been thinkin'
            'bout us, you know and...

The phone goes dead. Furious he slams it back
down, stalks back out to the sidewalk.

183     OMITTED

184     INT. TONY'S SEDAN - DAY

He gets in the driver's seat. The Shadow's next to him with the radio transmitter, Chi-Chi, in the back. Tony, seemingly unaffected by the weather, reaches for an open pint of ice cream, starts eating it with a plastic spoon. He alternates ice cream with coke through the scene; the dashboard of the car cluttered with cartons of half-eaten Chinese food.

The Shadow, disgusted with all this mess, restrains himself, staring out at the street with a hate-filled expression, saying nothing.

                    CHI-CHI
          (concerned)
          Everything okay Tony?


                    TONY
          Yeah roses. Where is this
          fuckin' guy? I don't got all
          day to piss away.


                    CHI-CHI
          Probably fucking his wife.
          (eating pizza)
          Jeezus it's cold.


185   THEIR POINT OF VIEW THROUGH TONY'S WINDSHIELD - DAY

          The door of the brownstone. No movement.
          Though now there's increasing traffic on
          the street and passing pedestrians.

                    TONY
          We oughta shoot him when he
          comes out the door, save a
          lotta bullshit.


186   INT. TONY'S SEDAN - DAY

                    CHI-CHI
          What's so important about
          this guy anyway? What's he
          a Communist?

                    TONY
          (snorting through his mouth)
          Nah he's no Communist. He's a
          kinda symbol, that's what he is.

                    CHI-CH1
          What the fuck's that mean --
          symbol?

                    TONY
          It's like when you die,
          your life meant something to
          somebody, y'know? It wasn't
          like you just lived it for
          yourself, but you did
          something for the rest
          of the human race too...

Tony snorts another line — seen through the
rearview mirror.

                    CHI-CHI
          (nods his head somberly)
          Yeah?

                    TONY
          Me, I wanna die fast. With my
          name written in lights all
          over the sky. Tony Montana. He
          died doin' it.

                    CHI-CHI
          Whatcha talking 'bout Tony,
          you ain't gonna die.

                              TONY
                    (doesn't hear him)
                    ...So I'll end up in a coffin.
                    So what? The cockroach fires
                    the bullet's gonna end up in a
                    coffin just like me. But I
                    lived better when I was here.
                    And that's what counts.

          Pause.

                              TONY
                    (nervous, to Ernie)
                    Ernie, what time?

                              ERNIE
                    Ten to.

                              TONY
                    (opening his door)
                    I gotta call Manny.

          He starts out the door. The Shadow barks out
          something in preemptory Spanish.

                              SHADOW
                    (Spanish)
                    Sit down!

                              TONY
                    Hey, you don't tell me what to
                    do, you...

                              CHI-CHI
                    Tony, he's coming!

     187  EXT. GUTIERREZ'S STREET - DAY

          Tony looks around, sees:

          Gutierrez coming out the door, briefcase in hand.

Tony gets back in the car.

188     THROUGH TONY'S WINDSHIELD - DAY

        Gutierrez gets into his sedan a quarter block
        down from his front door.

189     INT. TONY'S SEDAN - DAY

        Tony staring.

        The Shadow, most excited of all, like a
        panther that just spotted his prey, eyes
        alive for the first time.

190     THROUGH TONY'S WINDSHIELD - DAY

        Gutierrez sits there warming up his car,
        looking back at the brownstone.

191     INT. TONY'S SEDAN - DAY

                        SHADOW
                  (Spanish, excited)
                  The UN -- right in front of
                  it. In the daylight. That's
                  the way they want it.

        Tony breaks open a fresh vial.

                        TONY
                  (English)
                  Hey okay I don't give a shit
                  where, okay, you can blow him
                  up when you like okay, just
                  tell me okay — when you like.

        The chatter comes out jagged, irritating the
        Shadow who doesn't understand Tony's English
        anyway.

                              SHADOW
               (Spanish to Chi-Chi)
               What's he saying! You tell him
               stay inside thirty meters of
               the car okay -- no more you
               just stay inside thirty meters.

                              TONY
               (English)
               Hey okay I heard you the first
               time. One time okay. Just tell
               me one time.
               (snorts)

                              SHADOW
               (Spanish)
               I tell you thirty metres okay!
               You understand, madre de dios,
               why this hop-head is driving!

                              CHI-CHI
               Okay, okay.

                              TONY
               (English)
               Okay, okay, cool it willya all
               right.

192    THROUGH TONY'S WINDSHIELD - DAY

       Gutierrez pulls his car out of the parking space.

       Tony puts his car in gear, prepares to pull
       out when:

       Gutierrez stops his car, backs up — in the
       direction of his front door.

                              TONY
               What the --

206

Gutierrez comes to a halt, double-parked, honks.

193   INT. TONY'S SEDAN - DAY

                    TONY
              (to Chi-Chi)
              What's he doing? Where's he
              going?

194   GUTIERREZ'S BROWNSTONE - SIDEWALK - DAY

              The wife opens the door, steps out --
              followed, moments later, by two
              schoolchildren, books in hand. Gutierrez
              waves to them to come along.

195   INT. TONY'S SEDAN - DAY

              Tony looks astonished, back at Chi-Chi.

                    TONY
              What the fuck! You said the
              wife took 'em in the other car.

                    CHI-CHI
              She did boss. She did it every
              fucking day, I swear!

196   THROUGH TONY'S WINDSHIELD - DAY

              The two children are now climbing in the back
              of Gutierrez's sedan, the wife getting into the
              pasenger seat. They drive off.

197   INT. TONY'S SEDAN - DAY

              Tony, upset now, goes to his vial, snorts,
              turns sharply to the Shadow.

                    TONY
          Hey chico, no fuckin' way! No
          wife, no kids! We hit this
          fuckin' guy we hit him alone
          okay.

                    SHADOW
          (Spanish)
          No! Mr. Sosa says we do it
          now. We do it.

He has the strength of a born psychopath,
brooking no other reality but his own. He
stares a hole through Tony who gives way to
his intensity, going into a slow angry burn at
himself, putting the sedan in gear and going
after Gutierrez, muttering to himself.

                    TONY
          ...aw fuck this, this fuckin'
          asshole!

Chi-Chi, in the back, looks on worried.

198   NEW YORK STREETS - DAY - FOLLOWING GUTIERREZ'S SEDAN

          through Manahattan, towards the UN. The Shadow
          making the final adjustments on his decoder.
          He now sticks a key in it. A red light pulses
          at intervals.

          Tony, driving, glances, the tension building
          in him, he does another giant snort.

          Gutierrez's sedan, swerving out into traffic to
          pass a car, has a near collision with an
          insane bus driver and has to brake suddenly,
          angling into a deep pothole, shaking the car
          and honking angrily after the bus.

          The Shadow goes nuts, peering over the

dashboard to see if the bomb came loose.

>                   SHADOW
>           (to  himself, Spanish)
>           Madre de dios, my bomb! --
>           don't you fuckin' fall, my
>           little baby!

Perspiration starting to break out on his
forehead.

Tony also feels the sweat coming on.

>                   TONY
>           (muttering)
>           ...this is fuckin' crazy, man,
>           this is sloppy doing it this
>           way, you don't do it like
>           this...

He honks furiously at a cab that tries to cut
him off.

199    INT. TONY'S SEDAN - DAY

Tony, intense at the wheel, sneezing, his nose
running.

>                   SHADOW
>           (equally tense, in Spanish)
>           You're losing them! There!
>           That street, they go that
>           street!

>                   TONY
>           I see 'im! I see 'im!

>                   SHADOW
>           (Spanish)
>           Thirty metres! Thirty metres!
>           Go! Go!

                    TONY
             Shut the **fuck up**!

Honking like a madman and accelerating past a
truck...

                    TONY
             ...what am I doing? What the
             fuck am I doing here?...

200 THROUGH TONY'S WINDSHIELD - DAY

Gutierrez sedan pulling off at 47th and Second
Avenue heading for the United Nations building
which now appears at the end of the street.

201 INT. TONY'S SEDAN - DAY

                    SHADOW
             (Spanish)
             Okay, now... now. Right here.
             Easy. Easy!

The decoder.

Tony snorts.

                    TONY
             (muttering)
             Aw, fuck you, you fuckin'
             vulture...

The Shadow in stark profile. His finger
depresses the first key of the decoder.

202    UNDER GUTIERREZ'S CAR - DAY

       The bomb — pulsing red light.

203    THROUGH TONY'S WINDSHIELD - DAY

The Gutierrez sedan pulls off the sidestreet
into the thick of First Avenue traffic --
approaching the striking façade of the United
Nations.

204     INT. TONY'S SEDAN - DAY

The Shadow is in a full sweat.

                    SHADOW
            (Spanish)
            ...okay, okay, nice 'n'
            easy... at the corner... when
            he pulls up at the corner.

His finger hovering around the second key of
the decoder.

Chi-Chi in the back, leaning forward across
the seat.

                    TONY
            (muttering)
            Two kids in the car, Jesus
            Christ!

205     UNDER GUTIERREZ'S CAR - DAY

The bomb — jarred by a bump, pulsing red
light.

206     THROUGH TONY'S WINDSHIELD - DAY

Gutierrez' sedan inches its way out of the
traffic and eases along the curb.

207     INT. TONY'S SEDAN - DAY

Tony honking his way through traffic after
them, building to a climax with himself.

                    TONY
          (muttering)
          ...bunch of fuckin' vultures.
          You don't have the guts to
          look 'im in the eye when you
          kill him, you gotta hide, you
          fuckin' vulture.

Honk, honk.

                    SHADOW
          **Shut up!**

                    CHI-CHI
          (suddenly panicked)
          He's gonna get out! Hurry up,
          **hurry the fuck up!**

                    TONY
          (ignoring all the commotion)
          ...makes you feel good, hunh?
          Killing the wife and the kids.
          Big man. Well fuck you! What
          do you think I am? You think
          I'd kill two kids and a woman.
          Well **fuck that!** I don't **need**
          **that shit in my life.**

His face twisted in agony, he reaches down and
snaps his Baretta free from his ankle holster.
He swings it around sharply, leveling it on
the Shadow.

                    TONY
          **You** die, motherfucker!

The Shadow glances over at Tony, astonished.
Tony pumps two shots point-blank into him,
blowing his face off and smashing him against
the door of the moving sedan, blood and brains
splattering the windows and the seat covers.

                         CHI-CHI
                    Oh Jesus Christ! Jesus Christ!
                    What the...


               Tony swerving the sedan back across the
               Avenue, the traffic around them honking and
               moving along at its normal pace as the
               Shadow's body slumps down out of sight,
               another Monday morning traffic accident
               with blood and brains splattered up against
               a passenger window and nobody really sees...
               except a six-year-old girl in an adjacent
               vehicle; she wonders momentarily, then
               dismisses it.


                         TONY
                    (continuing to mutter)
                    ...so what'd you think I was,
                    hunh? A fucking worm like you!
                    I told you don't fuck with me!
                    I told you no kids! You
                    shoulda listened to me you
                    stupid fuck!


          CUT TO


208    OMITTED


209    EXT. JFK AIRPORT - THAT NIGHT

               Planes roaring.


210    INT. JFK AIRPORT

               Chi-Chi waiting in a busy lounge covering Tony
               on the phone; Tony's still wearing the same
               clothes with patches of blood on them.

                         TONY
                    Ernie? Where the fuck you been?

                    ERNIE'S VOICE
I had a delivery. Tony,
everything go okay, whatsa --

                    TONY
Fuck no? Where the hell's
Manny? I been calling all
over.

                    ERNIE'S VOICE
I don't know, Tony. He's been
gone last couple of days.
Didn't say nothing.

                    TONY
What! Where! I left that
sunufabitch in charge! What
the hell is going on here,
can't I trust anybody anymore.

                    ERNIE'S VOICE
I don't know, Tony, he just
took off, y'know, he didn't
say nothing... you all right?

                    TONY
No, I'm not all right. I'm
pissed off! And when I get
there I'm gonna kick some ass
all over the fuckin' place!

                    ERNIE'S VOICE
When you coming back, Tony?

                    TONY
Tonight!
(repeating to himself)
Where the hell is that
cocksucker? I can't trust
nobody no more. You think just
'cause I'm a nice guy...

                    ERNIE'S VOICE
            Uh, Tony, your mama called.
            Gina's gone. She got to see
            you right away.

                    TONY
            Gina's gone? Where! Oh fuck!
            Tell her I'll be there
            tonight. Okay?

                    ERNIE'S VOICE
            Right.

                    TONY
            (about to hang up, pauses)
            uh -- how 'bout Elvie — did
            she call?

                    ERNIE'S VOICE
            (a beat)
            No.

                    TONY
            Yeah, okay, okay... listen if
            she calls, tell her I love
            her, okay?

                    ERNIE'S VOICE
            Yeah, okay Tony.


        Tony hangs up. A moment of despair. Then he
        snorts another spoon and snaps back.

    CUT TO


211    EXT. AIRPORT - NIGHT

        Plane taking off.

    CUT TO

212   EXT. TONY'S MANSION - THAT NIGHT

>    Tony drives up in a white Corniche (the red
>    Jaguar having been shot to shreds earlier in
>    Lopez's attempt on Tony's life) with Chi-Chi,
>    jumps out in the same bloodstained clothes,
>    rushes in.

213   INT. TONY'S MANSION - NIGHT

>    Ernie meets them at the door.

>                    TONY
>          Hear from Manny?

>                    ERNIE
>          No Tony. Your mama called
>          again. She gotta see you. And
>          Sosa's been ringing every
>          half-hour on the eleven line.
>          Tony, he sounds pissed, he...

>                    TONY
>          Yeah, yeah, yeah... Chi-Chi,
>          get him on the line. In the
>          office.

>    Chi-Chi goes.

>                    TONY
>          What about Elvie -- anything?

>    Ernie shakes his head.

>                    TONY
>          You keep trying Manny. I need
>          that cocksucker, you hear, I
>          need him here! Okay?

>                    ERNIE
>          Right, Tony.

Tony stalks off, towards his office.

214     INT. TONY'S OFFICE

Amid his computer space games and half-dozen
televisions and  stereos, Tony picks up the
ringing phone.

                    TONY
            Yeah? Hi. Mami.

The other phone is ringing. Her voice on the
phone sounds hysterical and angry. Not really
listening, Tony breaks open a new vial, pours
the entire vial of coke out across the desk
into a thick quarter-moon pattern. He snorts.
Chi-Chi signals he's got Sosa on the other
line.

                    TONY
            (into the phone)
            Yeah, all right. I hear you.
            No problem, okay. I'll be
            there!

He hangs up, snorts, then pushes the button
Chi-Chi indicates. The telephone should be the
latest in gimmickry.

                    TONY
            ...so whaddaya say Alex?

Pause. The voice at the other end is very
controlled, very cold.

                    SOSA'S VOICE
            So what happened Tony?

                    TONY
            (casual)
            Oh we had some problems.

                    SOSA'S VOICE
          Yeah I heard.


                    TONY
          How'd you hear?


                    SOSA'S VOICE
          'Cause our friend gave a
          speech today at the UN. He
          wasn't supposed to give that
          speech.


                    TONY
          (shrugs)
          Yeah, well, your guy Alberto
          was a piece of shit, he didn't
          do what I said so I cancelled
          his fuckin' contract.


Pause at the other end.


                    SOSA'S VOICE
          ...my partners and I are
          pissed off.


                    TONY
          Hey Alex, no big deal. There's
          plenty other 'Albertos' so
          I'll deliver the goods next
          month.


                    SOSA'S VOICE
          (suddenly angry and letting
          Tony know)
          No! We can't do that. They
          found what was under the car,
          Tony. And our friend's got
          security now **UP the ass**. And
          the heat's coming down **hard** on
          me and my partners. There's

not gonna be a next time. You
blew it, **you fuckin' dumb
cocksucker!**

                    TONY
          Hey, you don't talk to me like
          that! Who do you ---

                    SOSA'S VOICE
               (simultaneous)
          I told you a long time ago,
          you little fuckin' monkey, not
          to fuck me and...

Tony holding the mouthpiece away from his ear
and talking at it like it was a face.

                    TONY
          Who the fuck you think you're
          talkin' to, hunh! Whatta you
          think I am? Your fuckin'
          slave! You don't tell me what
          to do, Sosa. You're shit! You
          want a war, you got it?

Slams the phone down.

                    TONY
          The fucking nerve of that guy!

In the cavernous silence of the room, he
listlessly turns to another line of coke.

     CUT TO

215    EXT. MIAMI STREETS - NIGHT

          Tony in the backseat in his white Corniche
          staring straight ahead. Ernie driving, Chi-Chi
          with him.

216    EXT. MOTHER'S HOUSE - SOUTHWEST MIAMI - NIGHT

The bulletproof white Corniche pulls up, Ernie
and Chi-Chi getting out first, checking the
street, Tony following quickly.

                    TONY
          (to Chi-Chi)
          You try Manny again. Gimme
          five minutes.

He hurries towards the house.

217    INT. MOTHER'S HOUSE - NIGHT

Mama is angry and ravaged with worry, made
weaker than previously, as if overhelmed by
events.

                    MAMA
          She got a place of her own,
          she don't tell me where. One
          day I follow her in a taxi.
          She goes into this fancy house
          in Coconut Grove.

                    TONY
          The Grove? Where'd she get
          that kinda money?

                    MAMA
          You! You were giving her the
          money, what do you think --
          don't you see what you do to
          her, don't you...

                    TONY
          I never gave her that kinda
          money.

                    MAMA
          Yes, you did! One time one
          thousand you gave her!...

                    TONY
          Mama, was there a guy with
          her?

                    MAMA
          I don't know, there was this
          other car in the driveway. I
          know if I went in there, she'd
          kill me, she's like you, she...

Tony's face filling with the old wrath, he
grips his mother by the shoulders.

                    TONY
          Where's this house, tell me!

                    MAMA
          Four hundred something. Citrus
          Drive. Four hundred nine. You
          gotta talk to her Tony, she
          don't listen to me anymore.
          She says to me 'Shut up! Mind
          your own business.' Exactly
          like you do to me. Ever since
          you come back, she's been
          getting this way.

He turns to leave but she clings to his arm.

                    MAMA
          Don't you see what you do to
          her? Don't you see? Why do you
          have to hurt everything you
          touch, why do you...

                    TONY
          (shakes himself loose, turns
          on her)
          No! You know why she left,
          Mama? Not 'cause of me. 'Cause
          of you.

                    MAMA
          Me?

                    TONY
          Yeah, it's you drove her nuts
          with your nagging and
          bitchin'.

                    MAMA
          (interrupts)
          Nagging and bitchin'? I only
          demand a little respect and
          dignity in this house, is that
          why I am nagging and bitchin'?

                    TONY
          (continuing)
          ...and you did the same thing
          to me. I wasn't this, I wasn't
          that -- never good enough for
          you. I never felt nothing from
          you, Mama -- nothing!

                    MAMA
          (interrupts)
          ...because I was putting food
          on the table, because I
          suffered for both of you...

                    TONY
          First time I ever needed you,
          where were you?

MAMA

Where was I?

TONY

...when I was in that Army jail in Cuba, rotting my ass off, **not once.** I hadda come out into the fuckin' streets to find out my mother and my sister are gone from my house, they left the country not one word, one letter, that's right. Where were you?

MAMA

(interrupts)
You... sin verguenza. From the time you were five, you gave me **heartbreak** and **humiliation** and **shame...**

TONY

That's right! That's right. What did you expect!

MAMA

(interrupts)
...that's what you brought into this house. If I were to listen to you, you would convert my house into your gangster headquarters...

TONY

...what do you expect now? To be loved? You got no love in you, Mama. What do you think Papi left for? And Gina? At least I didn't walk around with my head hanging down between my legs my whole

fuckin' life. Like Papi --
like the way you made Papi
feel. I made something outta
my life. I'm somebody and I'm
proud of it.

                    MAMA
          (interrupts)
          Somebody? You're proud? You're
          a nothing. You're an animal!

Tony storms out of the door as Mama pursues.

                    MAMA
          God help me, what have I done
          to you? You were a beautiful
          baby. I used to watch you
          sleep. So beautiful. How? How,
          Dios Santo, did you become
          such a monster, such an ugly
          little monster...

Tony slams the door, we hold a beat on her
face — as if she had finally answered her own
questions.


218    EXT. MOTHER'S HOUSE

          Tony stomps into his white Corniche, Ernie
          discreetly closing the door and getting in
          with Chi-Chi as Mama rips open her door in
          b.g. and stands there staring from the doorway --
          weeping and staring across the dark. Tony takes a
          strong hit of coke. The car whistles off.


       CUT TO


219    EXT. HOUSE - COCONUT GROVE - THAT NIGHT

          Tony in the backseat of the Corniche with
          Chi-Chi studies the house from across the

curb. It's quiet, rich, suburban, not calling
attention to itself.

Tony, seething, snorts another line of coke
laid out on the crystal bar dividing the
backseat, and revved, goes.

> TONY
> (to Chi-Chi)
> Wait here.

He approaches the front door, listening, the
hand sliding into his pocket. Inside a wistful
Billy Joel song plays over the stereo. He
rings a buzzer, waits.

Hold the pause. The door opens casually.
Standing there is Manny -- with a towel around
his waist.

> MANNY
> (surprised)
> Tony?

Tony stares, stunned.

Gina now comes into view behind Manny -- in a
bathrobe, a big smile of welcome for her
brother.

> GINA
> Tony!
> (eyes suddenly moving downward
> in alarm)

Tony with his Baretta pointed at Manny, his
expression filled with loathing.

Manny smiles easily and shrugs, the gesture
drawing Tony over the edge.

                    MANNY
          Hey Tony, c'mon we was...

The gun fires.

                    GINA
            Tony! No!

Tony fires a second time.

Manny slowly slumps downward against the
doorjamb, eyes on Tony, terribly surprised.

Tony holds the gun, staring down, separated
from himself.

Manny lies at his feet, dead.

                    GINA
            Manny!

She goes down to her knees, stunned out of her
mind, shakes him.

                    GINA
            Manny!

She looks up, insanely, at Tony, her eyes huge
with disbelief.

                    GINA
            You killed him?

Shaking her head at him incredulously.

                    GINA
          We got married just yesterday.
          We were gonna surprise you.

Tony stands there, doubly stunned by the news.

                              GINA
              Manolo, oh Manolo, what'd he
              do? What'd he do?


         She hugs his corpse tightly to her breast and
         makes horrible strangled sounds with her
         throat.

         Chi-Chi hurrying up to Tony, worried
         somebody's seen the shooting. Ernie follows.

                              CHI-CHI
              Tony, come on. We gotta get
              out of here.
              (to Gina)
              Come on baby... Gina!


         Suddenly she goes berserk.

                              GINA
              Noooooooooooo!


         And shoving Chi-Chi aside, launches herself on
         Tony, screaming incoherently like a madwoman,
         trying to kill him. She beats him around the
         head, the chest, scratches furrows of flesh
         from his face. He stands there, oblivious,
         numbed.

         Chi-Chi and Ernie have a demon on their hands.
         They manage at last to yank her off Tony,
         kicking and continuing to scream.

220      EXT. NANNY'S HOUSE - NIGHT

         Lights coming on in the houses around the
         neighborhood.

         Chi-Chi and Ernie, desperate now, drag her
         forcefully along the pavement into the
         Corniche. She continues to scream.

                    ERNIE
          (to  Chi-Chi)
          Get the body!

Tony, back at the door, looks down again.

The eyes of Manolo staring sightlessly.

Chi-Chi runs back, grabs Tony.

                    CHI-CHI
     Tony!

Pulls him. Tony snaps out of it.

                    TONY
          Yeah!

He goes. Chi-Chi lifting Manny's body, hauling
it.

Tony getting into the Corniche, Ernie pinning
Gina against the front seat. Chi-Chi propping
Manny into the driver's seat with him. The car
roars away.

The camera closing on Gina as she looks
through the glass partition of the Corniche,
at the slumped head of Manny in f.g., the
music surging unexorably.

                    GINA
          Manny! Manny! No!

     CUT TO


221  MIAMI STREETS - NIGHT

          The white Corniche whistles by like a hearse
          heading for hell.

222    EXT. TONY'S MANSION GROUNDS — THAT NIGHT

It goes roaring by the front gate and up the
driveway, gravel flying.

The camera curving to reveal two sedans
inching up the shadowed street, towards us,
their lights out. The cars stop. Eight men
emerge silently, blending into the shadows of
the trees.

223    INT. TONY'S MANSION - NIGHT

Tony, scratches across his face, strides
through the front door into the marble foyer.
Another Marielito is waiting for them at the
door.

Ernie and Chi-Chi are almost carrying Gina,
who is numb with shock.

                    CHI-CHI
        What do we do with her Tony?

                    TONY
        Do what? Where? Put her upstairs.
        Put her in my bedroom.
        (to Gina)
        It'll be all right, pussycat,
        you'll see everything'll be
        okay, I'll take care of you...

She looks up at him through her stupor and
spits in his face. Chi-Chi and Ernie pull her
away -- as Tony stares, upset but passive.
They trundle her up the stairs. Tony turns and
walks away.

224    INT. TONY'S OFFICE - NIGHT

Tony slumps on his couch. A haze of coke rises off the velvet like a snow scene painting on a Christmas card. Oblivious to the dust, he cuts open a fresh plastic kilo bag of coke and spreads the entire pound out across the black marble coffee table.

Ernie and Chi-Chi come in.

                    CHI-CHI
          We got some pills into her,
          she's cooling down.

Tony pays no attention, Ernie and Chi-Chi noticing the pile of coke.

Flashing his silver tooter, Tony snorts a truly giant amount in a large pendular swing of his elbow across the length of coffee table.

Pause as he lets it sink in.

                    CHI-CHI
          (worried)
          Boss, what we gonna do now?

                    TONY
          Do? We're gonna war that's
          what we gonna do. We gonna eat
          Sosa for breakfast. We're
          gonna close that fucker down.

Ernie and Chi-Chi sharing a look.

                    CHI-CHI
          (eyeing the coke)
          Hey Tony, why don't you go
          easy on that stuff, hunh?

Tony looks up at him, focuses. The eyes are uncompromising.

Ernie, a little scared of him now, turns away.
Chi-Chi follows.

Tony starts on another trek along the coffee
table.

CUT TO

225     EXT. TONY'S MANSION GROUNDS - LATER THAT NIGHT

The Bengal tiger paces his spot, restless.

A monsoon-like wind blows through the trees on
the estate.

The monkeys listen quietly.

The flamingoes flutter. Then there's a burst
of loud music from the stereo speakers on the
balcony -- a Billy Joel song, something smooth
and easy about the high times and how fast
they go...

...and we see Tony, in long shot, throw open
the terrace doors and stagger out onto the
balcony, overlooking his estate.

On a closer angle, we track him to the edge
of the balustrade. He's done so much coke now
he's practically catatonic; staggering and
muttering to himself.

                    TONY
          (insensate)
     ...Jesus fuckin' Christ whatsa
     matter with me, get a hold of
     y'self now these cocksuckers
     gonna run over you let 'em try
     I bury the cocksuckers...

His point of view -- panning his estate. The
dark emptiness echoes back at him. The wind
rustling the treetops. Tony shaking his head
at himself. He starts to cry.

                    TONY
          Ooooh fuck Manny, how the fuck
          did I do that? How the fuck!
          Oh Manny, Manny... you were
          there for me, you were the
          one, Manny, you understood,
          always understood... well what
          the hell happened, hunh? What
          the hell happened to us?...

In far b.g. now, behind Tony, on the video
monitors in his office we see:

The main gate and guard shack -- a Marielito
crosses into view, checks the gate, turns.
Suddenly two figures spring out at him. One of
them garrotting the Marielito. He struggles.

Another monitor now reveals two more figures
moving into the interior of the guard shack.
They knife the other Marielito.

A third monitor carries another image of
shadows moving through the trees on the
estate.

On the balcony, Tony is oblivious to it all,
spent, almost incoherent.

                    TONY
          ...I said to you, Manny, I
          said I never go crazy and you
          said, I would you sonofabitch
          and you was right... those
          were the good days hunh, we
          was crazy back in those days,

> we'd do anything, you and me,
> we was on the way up, nobody
> nothing coulda stopped us
> 'cause we were the best hunh —
> the fucking best...

As Tony turns and starts back through the
terrace doors into his study, the camera
glides around to a view of a hook flying up
and catching the balustrade. A shadow starts
climbing up as:

                    TONY
> ...we still are Manny, we
> still are -- see, I'm gonna
> wipe out all them fuckers out
> there, I'm gonna run the market,
> I'm gonna be King Cocaine you
> hear me, you buy you buy from
> me -- Tony Montana. Covers of
> all the magazines. Fan mail.
> Television stars, movie stars,
> shooting stars -- he's a
> star...

226    INT. TONY'S MANSION - OFFICE

As he crosses into his office, the camera
moves to reveal Gina standing there half-
dressed in the doorway, her eyes blazing
with hatred.

Tony sees her.

She steps forward, offering her body almost
naked to her brother.

                    GINA
> Is this what you want Tony?...

Tony shocked.

                    GINA
          You can't stand another man
          touching me. So you want me
          Tony, is that it? Well **here I
          am** Tony.


She fires the Baretta we now see in her hand.

The bullet grazes Tony in the leg, snapping
him from his catatonia as he goes reeling
across the floor behind his desk. She fires
again. Again.

                    GINA
          I'm all yours Tony, I'm all
          yours now.


Bullets ripping into the desk. She advances,
offering her sex, methodically shooting out
the clip at rhythmic intervals.

                    GINA
          Come and get me Tony. Before
          it's too late.


He spins across the desk, trying to put
distance between them. She sees him scurrying,
turns, an expression like a demented angel.

                    GINA
          Come on Tony, fuck me! Fuck
          me! Fuck me!


Advancing on him, firing. The furniture
tearing up, the chair spilling, television
sets and computer toys shattering, Tony
squirming away, hit again in the thigh,
shocked, scrambling over to the terrace
windows. Her next shot shatters the window
and as Tony ducks again to the side, we see
outside onto the terrace behind him:

A young Columbian punk no more than twenty --
one of the hitters -- is crouched there,
reacting to the broken window. He doesn't
hesitate, turning his machine gun on Gina.

Gina is torn to pieces by the firepower --
blown across the room, spine severed and
dead before she hits the floor.

Tony sees it, yells something, in the same
instant swivels to knock the barrel of the
machine gun aside. The punk is taken by
surprise, not having seen Tony, and Tony now
runs him backwards across the balcony and
hurls him over the balustrade.

The punk lands in one of the shallow pools on
the grounds at the base of the balcony.

Tony, from above, grabs up the punk's machine
gun and empties the whole clip into the figure
thrashing in the pool below.

Ernie runs into view on the far side of the
pool, spots Tony, yells up --

                    ERNIE
          Get outta here! Tony, they're
          everywhere!

Ernie suddenly wheels, hit in the face, by a
burst of silencer bullets.

We catch a brief glimpse of Sosa's black aide,
the Skull, moving quickly along the wall of
the house — directly underneath the balcony on
which Tony stands.

Tony, tossing the empty machine gun aside,
wildly runs back into his office to get more

guns, crosses to Gina's corpse. It takes him
by surprise. He comes to a dead stop, kneels,
looking questioningly in her face.

                    TONY
              (gently)
          Hey Gina come on, you still
          angry at me? I didn't mean to
          kill Manny, I was... I was...

Running his hands along her face, trying to
rouse her, gently lifting her eyelids.
Blood's running out of her mouth in rivers.

                    TONY
          Come on Gina, get off the
          floor. You're all dirty now,
          you need a bath... Mami's
          gonna be angry baby -- ooh is
          she gonna be mad at me! Come
          on open your eyes my baby,
          open your eyes - give me a
          smile.

There's been a steady pounding and calling now
on the door of the office. Tony finally hears
it, looks up, then over at the monitors. One
of them reveals Chi-Chi standing there outside
the door pounding it.

                    CHI-CHI
          Boss! Hey boss. Open up!

On the monitor we see Chi-Chi suddenly spin
and open fire down into the foyer. Return fire
decimates him. A grenade goes off, blows him
up against the door.

                    TONY
          Cheeee!

He now seems to come out of his catatonia,
runs to his sideboard, hauls out a shoulder-
fired rocket launcher and straps an Uzi across
his shoulder. He looks up at the monitor.

On the monitors, the hitters are now darting
across the foyer and coming up the left and
right hand stairs.

Three of them are already huddled outside the
door, around the corpse of Chi-Chi, motioning
to each other, laying a grenade at the base of
the door to blow it out.

Tony loading his rocket, intends to beat them
to the punch, talking to himself.

                    TONY
          So you wanna play hunh, say
          hello to my little friend
          here.

Karroooomph!

The rocket tears down the door and blows the
Columbian punks off the landing into the
foyer. It sounds like Armageddon, one of the
hitters screaming, smoke billowing wildly.

Tony, at the height of his mad glory, steps
out at the apex of the stairs, firing his
machine gun and yelling.

                    TONY
          Whores! Cowards! You think you
          can kill me with lousy bullets
          hunh?

He fires now. Left. Right.

Another hitter tumbles down the right-hand stair.

                    TONY
          Who you think I am? I kill all
          you fuckin' assholes. I take
          you all to fuckin' hell!

Left. Right.

Another hitter drops, screaming, off the
stairs into the pool below.

A grenade goes off. Tony is hit again, but
keeps on firing away. Laughing like a madman.

                    TONY
          You need an army you hear! An
          army to kill me!

Behind him we see the remainder of the pound
of cocaine go up in a burst of wind, whipping
around the office in auras of white. It is a
ghostly effect out of which now appears the
face of the Skull moving from the terrace
towards Tony's back with a sawed-off shotgun.

                    TONY
          Ha ha ha ha ha! You whores,
          you scum, I piss in your
          faces!!!! Ha ha ha ha ha!!

The Skull, now inches from Tony's back, pulls
the trigger and blows Tony's spine out his
belly.

Tony crashes forward over the bannister into
the interior swimming pool below.

He floats quietly face down in the lit blue
waters.

As the titles begin their crawl up, the music
theme is expressive salsa with a dash of
gaiety.

The camera moving off Tony to catch the
reflection of the lit sculpture on the
surface of the still waters. It says:

                "THE WORLD IS YOURS"

And so, for the brief moment, it was.

Our camera now distancing itself from the body
in the pool, panning past the dream villa,
past the shambles and the wealth, past the
hitters pillaging and looting and drawing that
obscene word "Chivato" in blood on the outside
walls, past the stacks of cash blowing across
the floor like leaves in autumn, with the
looters running after it across the busted
door with the tropic wind blowing down Coconut
Grove -- to the Miami skyline across Biscayne
Bay.

                    THE END

# SCARFACE ™

## THE MOVIE SCRIPTBOOK

Written by
Oliver Stone